ALL ABOARD AMERICA
CLASSIC AMERICAN TRAINS

EDITED BY
MELVILLE WHEATON

SMITHMARK

Page 1: The classic among the classics, Seaboard's *Orange Blossom Special* idles in the Ivy City Yards in the District of Columbia, circa 1939, shortly after steam locomotives were replaced with the powerful EMD diesel units.

Pages 2-3: Named for the legendary accumulator of empires, James Jerome Hill, Great Northern's *Empire Builder* was already a classic when the big EMD diesels went on line. The Great Northern's great one is seen here just east of Montana's Glacier National Park in 1947 during its early diesel days.

Below: The 1910 Baltimore & Ohio club car interior seen here is typical of those in service then on such classics as the *National Limited* and the *Capitol Limited.*

This edition published in 1995 by SMITHMARK Publishers Inc., 16 East 32nd Street New York, NY 10016

SMITHMARK books are available for bulk purchase for sales promotion and premium use. For details write or telephone the Manager of Special Sales, SMITHMARK Publishers Inc., 16 East 32nd Street, New York, NY 10016 (212) 532-6600.

Produced by Brompton Books Corp 15 Sherwood Place Greenwich, CT 06830

ISBN 0-8317-1452-2

Printed in China

10 9 8 7 6 5 4 3 2 1

TABLE OF CONTENTS

INTRODUCTION

Using the word 'classic' to describe North American trains conjures up memories of special trips on special trains bearing exotic names that spoke of power and glory and excitement. There was a time when trains had a life to them that was more than just the steel of their wheels and the mohair of their seat cushions. They had personalities. Boston & Maine's *Yankee Clipper* may have been physically identical to the *Puritan*, and the two may have even used locomotives interchangeably, but they were different. Each had a personality, and each personality was unique.

Some of the classic trains are now forgotten, while others will remain etched in the collective memory of North America forever. There is the memory of making a dawn trip to catch the *Zephyr*, of racing to the station to be on the *Rocket* when she pulled out in a big, humid cloud of steam.

The personalities were part and parcel of the excitement and memories. Who can forget traveling from New York to Chicago on the *Broadway Limited*? Or from Chicago to Los Angeles on the *Chief*? Then up the West Coast on the *Coast Daylight* or the *Coast Starlight*? Or across the entire breadth of Canada on the immortal *Canadian*? This book is a nostalgic celebration of those great trains, those great names and a truly great moment in American history.

In the earliest days of American railroading, trains had no specific names—except to people along the line—the

Above: **It was back in the middle 1920s, when this anonymous young woman would stand near the Baltimore & Ohio tracks outside Laurel, Maryland waiting to catch a glimpse of her one true love, an engineer on the classic *Capitol Limited*. Eventually they would wed, and she came to this spot no more.**

'mail train' and the 'accommodation.' If it was a line which had only one train a day each way, they were apt to be known as the 'Up Train' or the 'Down Train,' respectively. The oldest of the named trains was probably the Boston & Maine's *Up Portsmouth* and *Down Portsmouth*, which were obviously the two trains which shuttled between Boston, Massachusetts, and Portsmouth, New Hampshire. As faster trains became more numerous, there might be an occasional one known as 'the Express' or 'the Fast Mail,' such as those on the Burlington, the Great Northern and the Milwaukee roads. Many people think the name 'Limited' train implies a limited number of stops. However, the idea of a 'Limited' train was that of a sort of wager between railroad and passenger, who paid extra fare against the railroad's bet that it would arrive at the destination on scheduled time, or very nearly so. If not, the railroad would refund a part of the fare. That was the original idea, but the word 'Limited,' like 'Express' and 'Special,' came to be used very loosely.

The 'Limited' custom ended around the turn of the century, but there were still 'Limiteds' all over the country, as well as 'Specials' and 'Expresses.' As late as the 1950s, there were some 65 Expresses operating, including a *Pony Express* on the Union Pacific, along with about 57 Limiteds, some of which never really were Limiteds in the original meaning of the word. 'Flyer' was another rash boast. Trains cannot literally fly, but the name implied speed that was often not present. At least one 'Flyer'

averaged little more than 25 mph in its 285-mile run, even when it was on time! When the railroads began putting on what was regarded as a *very* fast train, a train that actually passed more than half of the stations along its course without stopping, it began to be informally called the 'Cannonball,' though the name was not originally printed on the timetable. The *Wabash Cannonball* was the most famous, although as late as the 1950s, there were four *Cannonballs* still running. These were not on just the Wabash, but the Norfolk & Western, the Boston & Maine and the Long Island as well!

The colorful names lent themselves to verse, and many of America's classic trains are remembered in song, such as the *Wabash Cannonball*. Then too, who will forget the train called the *City of New Orleans*? In the late 1970s, a generation after its heyday, there was even a Broadway musical starring the great Imogene Coca entitled *On the Twentieth Century Limited* that celebrated the train of that name.

The stories are several and conflicting as to the first officially named train. In the 1890s, the Central of Georgia for a time claimed precedence for its *Nancy Hanks*, which was named for the famous trotting horse foaled in the late 1880s. The *Nancy Hanks*, which was the fastest train in the South at the time, ran briefly in 1890-91, then faded away, but the Central of Georgia revived the name in the 1940s as the *Nancy Hanks II*. The Central even had a *Little Nancy*, which ran between Savannah and Augusta, and a *Man o' War* (named for the greatest of all race horses) for the 117-mile Columbus to Atlanta run. It was a rare combination of a diesel-drawn, air-conditioned local, with an observation-club car offering food and beverages, plus maid and porter service. The 1890s saw the beginning of many famous trains.

The Lehigh Valley's *Black Diamond Express* began in 1896, named of course for the anthracite coal which was that road's lifeblood.

Products of the region frequently played a role in identifying the trains that crossed it. The Reading had a *King Coal*, the St Louis & San Francisco (Frisco) had a *Black Gold* named for Oklahoma oil, the Bangor & Aroostook had a *Potatoland Special*, and the Pennsylvania & Southern had a *Peach Queen*, while the Seaboard Air Line operated a *Cotton Blossom*. In the Midwest, the Illinois Central had a *Hawkeye* and a *Land o'*

Corn, while the Rock Island had its immortal *Corn Belt Rocket*. And these were just the passenger trains.

Freight trains frequently carried nicknames that indicated their cargo. There was the *Coal Digger* on the Baltimore & Ohio and several *Paper Trains* on Canadian roads bringing newsprint to the United States. *Banana Specials* came out of the ports of Baltimore and Weehawken, through which came much of the supply of that fruit to the Northeast. The *Apple* on the Illinois Central came out of orchard country around Albert Lea, Minnesota. Two *Blue Gooses* originated in Florida on the Georgia & Alabama and the Georgia & Florida. There was also a *Bluenose* on the Canadian National. Two *Packers* which ran on the Chicago & Eastern Illinois hauled freight out of Chicago and on the Chicago & North Western out of Council Bluffs.

Pork Chops was an Illinois Central meat train out of Council Bluffs, and the *Textiler* ran on the Seaboard Air Line through the Carolinas. The *Bean Train* ran on the Southern Railway and the *Bean Extra* on the Atlantic Coast Line, both filled with Florida vegetables. The *Spark Plug* was a Southern Railway freight that carried motor vehicle parts from Cincinnati to Atlanta. The *Cabbage Cutter* and *Fruit Block* were Western Pacific freights out of California's Central Valley, and *Gas Wagon* ran on the Pennsylvania Railroad out of Detroit. The Chicago & North Western even had a cereal train out of Cedar Rapids known to the personnel as *Mush*.

When the Southern Railway announced its *Textile Special* from Southern cotton mills to New York, the operatives promptly renamed it *Boll Weevil*. The Norfolk & Western's *Camel Special* needs no further identification of the product that it carried out of Winston-Salem, North Carolina.

Then, too, many of the classic American trains were named for their point of origin or their destination. There was the *Akronite* on the Pennsylvania, the *Bostonian* on the New Haven, and the *Chicagoan* on the Santa Fe, Canadian National and New York Central. The *Cincinnatian* was on the Baltimore & Ohio, the *Clevelander* ran on the Pennsylvania, the *Detroiter* on the New York Central and the *Houstonian* on the Missouri Pacific ('MoPac'). The *Miamian* ran on the Pennsylvania and the Richmond, Fredericksburg & Potomac, and the *Nashuan* ran on the Boston & Maine. There were three

New Yorkers on the Delaware, Lackawanna & Western, New Haven and Pennsylvania, the *Orleanean* ran on the MoPac, the *Pittsburgher* on the Pennsylvania, the *San Diegan* on the Santa Fe, the *Scrantonian* on the Delaware, Lackawanna & Western, the *Shreveporter* on the Kansas City Southern, the *Trojan* on the Boston & Maine between Boston and Troy, and the *Tulsan* on the Santa Fe. There were two *Washingtonians* taken out of that city by the Pennsylvania and the Baltimore & Ohio, respectively. Canadian National, the big government-owned line, had trains named for many Canadian destinations. These included the *Manitoba Limited*, the *Winnipeg Limited*, the *Ontario Limited*, the *Saskatchewan Express*, the *Quebec*, the *Toronto* and both a *Montreal* and a *Montrealer*.

There were also regional appellations, including an *Easterner*, a *Southerner*, a

Above: **During the 1920s, the Baltimore & Ohio's *National Limited*, sister train to the *Capitol Limited* seen opposite, offered the services of a Train Secretary in a quiet corner of the club car.**

10

Below: During the halcyon days of the great classic trains, the railroads decorated the dining cars, club cars and even the rooms and 'roomettes' thematically in an attempt to capture a particular ambience.

Seen here is an advertising agency's fanciful rendering of the French Quarter Lounge aboard Southern Pacific's *Sunset Limited.* New Orleans was the eastern terminus of this classic route, and the Lounge was designed to make you feel that you had already arrived.

New Englander and several state citizens, such as the *Coloradoan*, a *Dakotan*, a *Georgian*, a *Kansan*, an *Idahoan*, a *Kentuckian*, a *Marylander*, a *Texan* and even an *Ozarker*. The *Sooner* on the Missouri, Kansas & Texas was the one who jumped the gun in the Oklahoma land rush. There were three *Westerners*—one of them, believe it or not, on the Boston & Maine.

College towns were immortalized by the *Dartmouth* on the Boston & Maine and two *Varsitys* on the Chicago, Milwaukee & St Paul through Madison, Wisconsin, and on the Cincinnati, Indianapolis & Western through Bloomington, Indiana.

The time of day played a part in the naming of many trains. The New York, New Haven & Hartford had both *Day* and *Night Cape Codders* and the *Sundown*, while the Boston & Maine had a *Day White Mountain*. There were two *Twilights* on the Delaware, Lackawanna & Western and New York Central, several *Midnights*, the Illinois Central's *Night Diamond*, an *Overnighter* each on the New Haven and Boston & Maine, Southern

Pacific's *Starlight* and *Daylight* and the New Haven's *Night Cap*. The Illinois Central also had a *Daylight*, and there were numerous trains identified as the *Midnight Special*, including the New York Central's Cincinnati to Cleveland service. Such a name is far more appealing than the airline term 'red eye.' There is magic in the word 'night.' Could there be a prettier, more fitting name for a sleeping car than the New Haven's *Nightfall*— with the same road's *Nightvale* and the Pennsylvania's *Nocturne*?

Three official state animals were honored. The *Badger Express* and *Gopher* were both on the Great Northern, and the *Wolverine* on the New York Central. Then there were birds, such as the *Blue Bird* on the Wabash, the *Flamingo*, which ran upon the tracks of the Louisville & Nashville, the Central of Georgia and the Atlantic Coast Line. There was a train on the Kansas City Southern and the Louisiana & Arkansas called the *Flying Crow* because of its directness. From March 1930, the *Gull* served the Boston & Maine and on the Maine Central, continuing into Canada on Canadian National. The

Humming Bird ran on the Chicago & Eastern Illinois and Louisville & Nashville, the *Kentucky Cardinal* on the Illinois Central, the *Lark* and the *Oakland Lark* on the Southern Pacific, the *Meadow Lark* on the Chicago & Eastern Illinois, the *Nightingale* on the Chicago & North Western and the *Pelican* on the Pennsylvania, Norfolk & Western and Southern. There were also three *Oriole*s and two *Hawkeye*s in Iowa.

There was a flock of *Eagle*s on the Missouri Pacific and its subsidiary, the Texas & Pacific. These included the venerable *Aztec Eagle*, along with the *Colorado Eagle*, *Delta Eagle*, *Missouri River Eagle*, *Valley Eagle*, *Louisiana Eagle* and *Texas Eagle*. Four roads—the Southern Pacific, the New Haven, the Lackawanna and the Canadian National—ran *Owls*, and the Boston & Maine had a *Night Owl*.

'Dog' was a favorite epithet for crawlers made up of cast-off equipment of the parent road which covered only a few miles daily out and back. 'Short Dog,' 'Hound Dog,' 'Bulldog' and 'Runt' were insults with a certain similarity. There is a well-known legend that the famous

Above: **During the 1920s, the Baltimore & Ohio's *National Limited*, sister train to the *Capitol Limited* seen opposite, offered the services of a Train Secretary in a quiet corner of the club car.**

Below: The Pullman Company produced the passenger cars that ran on nearly every railroad in the United States. Named for the Revolutionary War heroine (whose real name was Mary Ludwig Hays McCauley), the *Molly Pitcher* was a dining car on the Baltimore & Ohio.

According to popular legend, but unsupported by fact, George Pullman's daughter Florence named every Pullman car. As the story went, her father started out paying her a dollar a car when she was a little girl, and eventually paid her more than $500.

Elvis Presley song *You Ain't Nothin' But A Hound Dog*, in which a person is compared derogatorily to a 'hound dog,' actually refers to a local on the Gulf, Mobile & Ohio known informally as the *Hound Dog*!

Another colorful, informal nickname originated with the fact that the sale of alcoholic beverages was—and still is for that matter—prohibited in certain states. The nickname was hung upon an Illinois Central train which ran from 'dry' Kentucky to 'wet' Cairo, Illinois, carrying citizens intent on replenishing their stocks of liquor. The train's very apt nickname was *Whiskey Dick*, after one of Bret Harte's most comically memorable characters. This name was later transferred to an Illinois Central freight train running out of Louisville, in delicate allusion to the quantities of bourbon produced in that city, the largest in a state where most of the counties were 'dry.'

Individual cars also were memorable by their names. When George M Pullman remodeled a Chicago & Alton coach into his first sleeping car in 1859, he gave no thought of *naming* her, or really to the matter of how his cars were to be designated. He just let that first one remain under its old Alton appellation 'Number 9.' When he built his first car from rail to roof in 1865, he called it Car A, but thought of it informally as the *Pioneer*. Greatly underestimating the growth of his business, he began lettering his cars, A, B, C, but found that he would soon be down to Z, with nowhere else to go. He

thought of using numbers, but this would have interfered with the railroads' own coach numbers, so Pullman was driven to using names.

Pullman was not the first in the business of supplying passenger cars to the railroad companies, though he seems to have been the one who introduced the naming of cars. John Webster Wagner, a former New York Central Station agent, remodeled a baggage car into his first sleeper in the late 1850s. Commodore Vanderbilt of the New York Central loved the idea, and for years he supplied some formidable opposition for Pullman.

In 1868, another important rail car builder, the Wagner Palace Car Company, introduced the first two parlor cars, *Catskill* and *Highlander*—each including three bedrooms—on the New York Central. Pullman quickly took up this idea of cars that would both sleep *and* feed their passengers, and he called them 'hotel cars.' Pullman's first hotel car, the *President*, which was put in service between Buffalo and Detroit in 1866, was a 75-foot-long section sleeper with a small kitchen in one end, from which a chef and two 'porter-waiters' dispensed hot meals on folding tables set after the berths had been stowed for the day.

The clashes that might have been expected between persons in the same section who wanted early breakfast and those who preferred to sleep late did not seem to be great deterrents to their popularity, and Pullman promptly built two more hotel cars, the *Western World* and

the *Viceroy*. The *Western World* reportedly had a wine cellar. Following these, the *City of Boston* and *City of New York* were built. They surpassed all others in elegance, but cost more than $30,000 apiece in 1870 dollars. Today, that would be close to $10 million. Two additional hotel cars, *Arlington* and *Revere*, were built explicitly for the Boston Board of Trade's excursion from Boston to San Francisco in 1870, but thereafter the production of such lavish vehicles slowed down. Hotel cars, though fewer, continued into the 1890s, when they were apt to be named for famous hotels, such as *St Nicholas* and *Gilsey*. Some dining cars were named for noted chefs, with names such as *Savarin*, *Aberlin* and *Valentin*.

The first Pullman-built dining car appeared on the Chicago & Alton in 1868, and of course was named *Delmonico*, after the ultra-chic New York restaurant that was at the apogee of the dining experience in the American mind during that era. Strangely, Europe was introduced to luxury cars by *Americans*. Pullman had actually begun operating sleeping and parlor cars in England by 1873. In that same year, Colonel WD Mann, publisher of the Mobile, Alabama *Register*, founded the Mann Boudoir Palace Car Company. With his 'boudoir palace cars,' Mann introduced the European continent to sleepers on the line between Vienna and Munich. The Mann cars were divided transversely into 'boudoirs,' each entered directly from the sides, and connected by private doors to which

'only the porter' carried a key. These cars were the ultimate in silken elegance, and soon equivalent parlor cars appeared in America with names such as *Adelina Patti*, *Marie Antoinette* and *Fontainebleau*.

Julius George Medley, a British tourist in 1872, was greatly impressed by American parlor cars. 'By paying an extra dollar for about every 200 miles,' he said, 'you can have a seat in a luxurious saloon, with sofas, armchairs, mirrors and washing rooms and the inevitable spittoons.'

As early as the late 1880s, geography became less prevalent in certain quarters and trains were named *Morning Star*, *Evening Star*, *Lone Star*, *Twilight*, *Olive Branch*, *Wild Rose* and *Monte Cristo*. Pullman supplied and owned the cars, but the company let their clients—the railroads where they ran—have a voice in the naming.

Pullman cars were not the first cars in the railroad world to be named, just like ships. Before or at about the same time

Above: **Built in 1868, and running on the Chicago & Alton, the original dining car *Delmonico* was named for the most fashionable restaurant in New York City, whose fame was well-known nationwide.**

Indeed, there were restaurants as well as dining cars throughout North America that 'borrowed' this legendary appellation.

when Pullman began naming sleepers, Daniel Torrance—one of the several sons-in-law of Commodore Cornelius Vanderbilt who built the New York Central and who served as superintendent of that road for several years—had one of the earliest private cars ever seen in America. It was painted a dark brown with its name, *Shoo Fly*, in a scroll on its side, the 'Shoo' in gilt letters, followed by a picture of a fly in red. The Commodore himself announced his presence in the hinterland by the name 'Vanderbilt' on his private car. Adolphus Busch, the marketing genius who built his St Louis brewery into one of the world's largest, rode around in a coach that he modestly named *Adolphus*. Busch even had a private railroad for delivering his beer, and which pulled *Adolphus* on demand.

In the latter decades of the century, private cars, intended to serve as rolling homes for 12 to 18 vacationers or perhaps a famous stage star with his or her select company, or maybe just one lucky traveler in a lonely, undisturbed state, with a staff to gratify every wish, were proffered by both the Pullman and Wagner car companies. Their names hinted at carefree roaming. *Arcadia, Utopia* and *Riviera* rolled in the 1880s, and were followed by *Wanderer, Traveler, Idler, Idlewild* and *Newport*, as well as those named after French and English light operas such as *Olivette* and *Iolanthe*. On a completely different subject, Pullman also had cars dubbed *Izaak Walton* and *Davy Crockett*, for hunting and fishing parties, with kennels for dogs, racks for guns and chefs especially skilled in broiling fish and game.

Until the turn of the century and even later, a legend persisted that Pullman's daughter Florence—later Mrs Frank Lowden—named every car. As the story goes, she began as a small girl, receiving a dollar per name from her father, which rose in popular myth to $100, $500 and even $1000. The climax of the legend was reached when she was placed on a flat salary of $20,000 a year. The truth of the matter, according to a memo issued by the company in the 1940s, is that she never named a single car. The 'official' story is that a committee of Pullman managers was given the task of naming the cars.

When five sleepers were completed in 1866 for what was soon to be the Chicago, Burlington & Quincy, they went far afield and chose *Atlantic, Pacific, Aurora, Omaha* and *City of Chicago*, but that soon

Above: **While its detractors would wince at the term 'classic' used in the same sentence as the name 'Amtrak,' the American National Rail Passenger Corporation (Amtrak) today uses many of the great classic names on its routes. In fact, the Amtrak Superliners provide a pleasant travelling experience, although the schedules are much more sparse than in the golden years of North American rail travel.**

Left: **Canadian Pacific's *Canadian* crosses the Stoney Creek Bridge in British Columbia, circa 1965. Just a few years later, as Amtrak was assuming the great United States routes, this classic Canadian route would be taken over by VIA Rail Canada.**

Above: **Powered by an EMD E2 unit, the classic *City of San Francisco* crosses the Great Salt Lake causeway, circa 1940.**

Below: **Classic Pullman boudoir accommodations, circa 1927.**

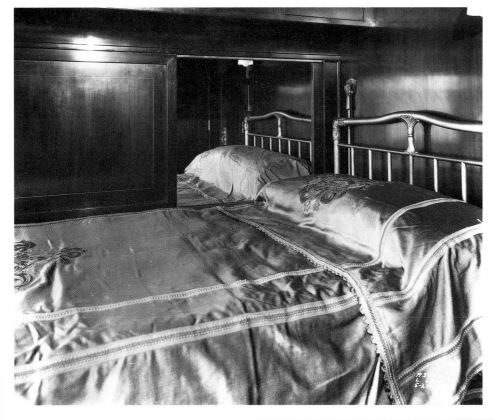

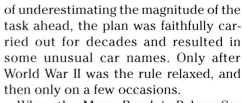

changed. With the exception of a few classical and literary words, the early sleepers were nearly all given geographical names, drawn mostly from the area in which the cars were operated. In the beginning, Pullman had decided that no name should ever appear on more than one car. While this was another example of underestimating the magnitude of the task ahead, the plan was faithfully carried out for decades and resulted in some unusual car names. Only after World War II was the rule relaxed, and then only on a few occasions.

When the Mann Boudoir Palace Car Company was taken over by Pullman in 1889, there were just a few duplicates of Pullman names on its cars. However, when the Wagner Palace Car Company was absorbed by Pullman in 1899, no less than 300 of its car names, mostly geographical, were found to be duplications of those on Pullman cars. Something had to be done, and done quickly. Richmond Dean, Pullman's 'vice-president in charge of nomenclature,' had a friend who was the city librarian of Chicago. The librarian consented to admit a squad of researchers from the Pullman offices into the library at night. Into the small hours of the morning they dug deep into ancient history and the classics, coming up with names, some of which twisted the tongues of travelers and porters for long afterward. These included *Antiphon, Archimedes, Belsarius, Berosus, Circe, Demosthenes, Diogenes, Hesiod, Hippocrates, Hyperion, Stamonides* and *Theocritus*, to name but a few.

Many of the classic passenger trains had disappeared before World War II,

such as the Alton's *Hummer* and *Night-hawk*, the Chicago Great Western's *Red Bird* and *Blue Bird*, and North Western's Omaha to Minneapolis/St Paul *Nightingale*. However, the Pennsylvania's *Congressional Limited*, the Union Pacific's *Overland Limited*, the Southern Pacific's *Sunset Limited*, the Santa Fe's *California Limited*, the Alton's *Midnight Special*—remembered as a real 'hotel on wheels'—the Baltimore & Ohio's *Royal Blue Flyer* and the New York Central's *Knickerbocker* were still running as late as the 1950s.

In the days when train travel was still a wonderful experience, taking the *Limited*, the *Rocket* or the *Bullet* came to be a way of life. One seemed to derive a certain persona from the train one took regularly. This writer remembers an uncle who always arrived on the *Senator*, and I was practically in my teens before I realized that he was a wine salesman and not really an actual senator.

By the mid-1950s, the magic was gone. My uncle now arrived in a Buick and the excitement of taking the *Cannonball* was reduced to the drudge of Flight 1054. The interstate highway system was completed and air travel became faster, safer and more efficient. The railroad companies quickly abandoned their passenger service, which they claimed had never *really* been profitable.

In 1970, as rail passenger service had all but vanished, the United States Congress created the National Railroad Passenger Corporation (Amtrak) by the Rail Passenger Service Act. According to the provisions of the act, railroads could discontinue their passenger service if they turned over passenger equipment to Amtrak. Most American railroads, suffering disastrous losses from passenger service, agreed. Beginning in 1971, Amtrak began operating the first nationwide passenger service in the United States.

Top: **The classic *City of Los Angeles* was operated jointly by both the Union Pacific and the Chicago & NorthWestern.**

Above: **An early streamlined Union Pacific diesel pulling the *City of San Francisco* across the Rockies, circa 1936.**

Above: Canadian Pacific's classic *Dominion* glides across a snow-covered landscape along the Bow River in Alberta, circa 1939.

Notable exceptions were the Denver & Rio Grande Western, the Rock Island and the Southern Railway. However, the Denver & Rio Grande Western discontinued its last passenger service in 1983, agreeing to an assumption of passenger service on its Denver to Salt Lake City route by Amtrak. The Rock Island went bankrupt in 1980 and the Southern turned over operation of its last passenger train to Amtrak in that same year. In Canada, VIA Rail Canada was created in 1977 for much the same purpose as Amtrak was in the United States. In 1978, VIA took over Canada's two great transcontinental routes, Canadian National's *Super Continental* and Canadian Pacific's *Canadian.*

The only track owned and operated by Amtrak is the Boston-New York-Wash-

ington Northeast Corridor. All other tracks, with the exception of a former New York Central section between Porter, Indiana, and Kalamazoo, Michigan, are owned and operated by the original freight-hauling railroads, a circumstance that limited Amtrak's efforts to increase the speed and frequency of service on its routes other than the Northeast Corridor.

Through Amtrak and VIA, some semblance of the old magic is still alive on North America's rails. One can still set out from Chicago to Seattle on the *Empire Builder*, to San Francisco on the *California Zephyr*, or to the Gulf Coast on the *City of New Orleans*, and one can still go to sleep to the gentle rocking of the *Coast Starlight* and dream of those wonderful bygone days of the classic trains.

CANADA

Above: **Making its maiden run in July 1836, Canada's first train was pulled by the *Dorchester*, a straight-stacked 0-4-0 similar to Robert Stephenson's *Rocket*, the world's first practical high-speed locomotive, which had gone into service in England seven years before.**

Facing page: **Canadian Pacific's classic *Canadian* snakes its way along the Bow River in the Rockies, circa the 1960s.**

Originally operated by the Canadian Pacific Railway, the *Canadian* was probably the greatest of all the classic Canadian passenger routes. The great streamliner made its inaugural run on the relatively late date of 24 April 1955, offering the longest dome car train ride in the world—a distance of 2905 miles—from Montreal to Vancouver. With its Scenic-Dome cars, a whole realm of sightseeing was opened up. Passengers could view the lush Canadian landscape better than ever before. Lakes, prairies and spectacular mountain vistas now seemed to envelope them. In addition, the

Canadian provided excellent dining facilities, plush sleepers and a full range of passenger amenities. Currently operated by VIA Rail Canada, the *Canadian* (in French, *Canadien*) is still the proud heir to a long tradition of North American *trains deluxe*, and is one of the comprehensive rail travel offerings of Canada's nationalized passenger system, VIA Rail Canada. The *Canadian* now makes a journey of 2776 miles through some of the most scenic and awe-inspiring landscape that Canada has to offer.

Canadian Pacific's rival, Canadian National, was the government-owned 'Grand Trunk' of Canada, the biggest railroad in the country and, indeed, in all of North America. One of Canadian National's first classic streamliners was the *Maritime Express*, which first made its Montreal to Halifax, Nova Scotia, run on 1 March 1898. The *International Limited* linked Montreal with Chicago on 24 June

1900, and the *Ocean Limited* was added to the Montreal to Halifax route in the summer of 1904. By 1912, Canadian National's menu of great trains included the *Alberta Express* connecting Winnipeg, Manitoba, with Edmonton, Alberta; the *Lake Superior Express* linking Winnipeg with Duluth, Minnesota; and two trains linking Manitoba's capital with St Paul, Minnesota (and with the Great Northern and Northern Pacific), the *Winnipeg Limited* and the *Manitoba Limited*.

Canadian Pacific's service to the prairies from the *west* included the Vancouver to Medicine Hat (via Calgary) trains the *Kettle Valley Express* and the *Kootenay Express*.

The summer of 1914 saw the inauguration of an interlocking set of classic streamliners that linked Canada's population centers with the prairies and the west coast. The gleaming new *National* ran from Toronto to the hub in Winnipeg,

Below: Canadian National's *Super Continental*, seen here near Yale British Columbia in 1955, was this railway's preeminent transcontinental service.

and from there a traveler could take the *Coast Limited* to Vancouver. In July 1916, the *National*'s route was integrated with that of the *Atlantic* to provide direct service from Winnipeg to Quebec City.

The finest of all Canadian National's class streamliners, the *Continental Limited*, entered service between Montreal and Vancouver on 3 December 1920. Replaced by the *Super Continental* on 24 April 1955 in response to Canadian Pacific's *Canadian*, this train remains one of the most memorable in the pantheon of Canadian classics. The *Canadian* was itself a successor to Canadian Pacific's venerable *Dominion*, while the name *Canadian* had earlier been assigned to the Canadian Pacific joint venture with the New York Central between Chicago and Montreal.

On 12 March 1923, Canadian National established its Passenger Traffic Department to coordinate the activities of its own main line service as well as the passenger service of smaller roads that had been merged into the government-owned system. Over the next three years, a number of new services were added, including the Ottawa to Toronto *Capitol City*, the Toronto to Haliburton *Highlander*, the Regina to Prince Albert *Owl*, the Montreal to Quebec City *Citadel*, *Montreal* and *Quebec*, and the Ottawa to Toronto *Queen City*. During the third week of June 1927, Canadian National launched two major lines, the Halifax to Montreal *Acadian* and the Toronto to Vancouver *Confederation*. The latter served as a complement to the *Continental Limited*.

The expansive 1920s also saw the inauguration of most of Canadian National's great international routes, many of which were offered in partnership with American roads on whose tracks and behind whose locomotives the trains ran south of the border. There was the Montreal to Boston *New Englander*, the Halifax to New York *Down Easter*, the Montreal to Detroit *Eastern Flyer* and the *Mount Royal* (English for 'Montreal') that connected that city with Boston and New York.

The two appropriately named classic Washington to Montreal streamliners, the southbound *Montrealer* and the northbound *Washingtonian*, made their first runs on 14 and 16 June 1924, respectively. Three trains between Montreal and Chicago went into service in the 1920s. These were the *Chicago Express* in January 1924, the *Inter-City Limited* in

Above and opposite: **The Vista Dome on the Canadian Pacific** *Canadian* **offered perhaps the most fabulous alpine views of any main line train in North America. The crossing of the Stoney Creek Bridge, as seen here, was always a highlight of the run to or from Vancouver. It was literally the most breath-taking quarter-mile on the Canadian Pacific.**

June 1926 and the fabled *Maple Leaf,* which made its maiden run on 15 May 1927.

The lucrative New York to Chicago run was the scene of a spirited rivalry between the New York Central's *Twentieth Century Limited* and the Pennsylvania Railroad's *Broadway Limited.* On 27 April 1924, Canadian National entered the competition with its westbound *Chicagoan* and eastbound *New Yorker.* The latter train used Canadian National trackage to compete with the American giants.

For two decades after the 1920s, which saw the inauguration of more classic Canadian trains than any other era, relatively few new trains were put into service. This was partly because of the global depression of the 1930s and World War II in the 1940s, but it was also due to the fact that the Canadian network was largely in place by 1929.

Outstanding Canadian National trains that began service in the 1930s included the *Jasper Park Special,* which began its run from Chicago to Vancouver by way of Jasper, Alberta, at the head of the Canadian Rockies on 10 January 1932. Then there was the *Gull* that connected Boston with the Maritimes, and the *Maine Coast Express* that began running from Montreal to Kennebunkport, Maine, on 29 April 1934. There were also a number of short runs out of the hub in Toronto. The *Toronto* began running to Buffalo in 1930, and the *Northland* began service to Timmins and the *Toronto Express* to London in 1937. Another classic Montreal to Chicago service, the *La Salle,* also began in 1937. The Montreal to Halifax, Nova Scotia, service, the *Scotian,* dates to 16 March 1941 during the darkest days of World War II.

After the war, it was nearly a decade before Canadian National got down to the business of adding a systematic program of new lines to address the new realities of competition from airlines and automobiles. However, in the early 1950s

CANADIAN PACIFIC RAILWAY
WORLD'S GREATEST TRAVEL SYSTEM

THROUGH CAR SERVICE.
Coaches on all trains unless otherwise noted.

ABBREVIATIONS: — Sec.—Section; D.R.—Drawing-room; Cpt.—Compartment; D.B.R.—Double Bedroom; S.B.R.—Single Bedroom.

Train Nos. 1 and 2.

Colonist.........Montreal and Winnipeg.
Tourist Sleeper..Winnipeg and Moose Jaw—13-Sec.
    ★Calgary and Vancouver—13-Sec.
Parlor........★Montreal to Ottawa.
    ★Calgary and Vancouver. ★Kenora and Calgary.
Restaurant Sleeper..★Montreal and Fort William—6-Sec., 1 D. B. R.
    (Open Fort William 10.00 p.m.)
Sleepers......★Winnipeg and Regina—8-Sec., D.R., 2 Cpt. (Open
    Regina 9.15 p.m. and to 8.00 a.m.)
    ★Winnipeg and Moose Jaw—8-Sec., 4 D.B.R.
    ★Calgary and Vancouver—12-Sec., D.R. (Open Calgary
    10.00 p.m.)
    ★Montreal and North Bay—12-Sec., D.R. (except Sat.).

Nos. 3 and 4—THE DOMINION—Toronto and Vancouver.

Observation Lounge Sleeper..★Toronto and Vancouver—D.R., 3 Cpt.
Sleepers......★Toronto and Vancouver—12-Sec., D.R.
    ★Toronto and Vancouver—10 Roomettes, 5 D. B. R.
    ★Toronto and Vancouver—8-Sec., D.R., 2 Cpt.
    ★Fort William and Winnipeg—12-Sec., D.R. (In Trains
    3 or 7 Fort William to Winnipeg) (open 10.00 p.m.)
(Sleepers Toronto open 10.00 p.m.)
Tourist.......★Toronto and Vancouver—14-Sec. (In Train 5 Toronto to
    Sudbury, thence Train 3.)
Diner........★Toronto and Vancouver.

Nos. 7 and 8—THE DOMINION—Montreal and Vancouver.

Obs. Solarium Sleeper..★Montreal and Vancouver—4 D.B.R., 1 Cpt.
Cpt. Sleeper..★Montreal and Vancouver—10 Cpt.
Sleepers......★Montreal and Vancouver—12-Sec., D.R.
    ★Winnipeg to Vancouver—12-Sec., D.R.
    Winnipeg to Vancouver—12-Sec., D.R.
    ★Ft. William to Winnipeg—12-S., D.R. (In Trains 3 or 7.)
    ★Sudbury to Montreal—12-Sec., D.R. (open 9.00 p.m.)
    ★Regina and Lethbridge—12-Sec., D.R. (except Saturday
    from Regina, except Sunday from Lethbridge).
Tourist.......★Montreal and Vancouver—14-Sec.
Parlor Car (except Sunday)..★Ottawa to Montreal.
Diner.... ...★Ottawa to Vancouver. ★Vancouver to Montreal.

THE DOMINION.
No. 9—Montreal to Sudbury. (Daily.)
No. 5—Toronto to Fort William (except Sunday).

Sleeper.......★Montreal to Sudbury—12-Sec., D.R., (open to 8.00 a.m.).
Tourist.......★Toronto to Vancouver—14-Sec. (In No. 5
    Toronto to Sudbury, thence in train No. 3.)
Buffet Parlor Car (Daily)..★Montreal to Ottawa.
Parlor........★Montreal to Ottawa (except Saturday).
    ★Montreal to Ottawa (Sunday).

THE DOMINION.
No. 10—Sudbury to Montreal. Daily.

Buffet Parlor (Daily) Parlor (except Sunday)..★Ottawa to Montreal.

Nos. 3-13-7 and 8-14-4—SOO DOMINION.

Sleeper.......★St. Paul and Calgary—8-Sec., 1 D.R., 2 Cpt.
Tourist.......★St. Paul and Moose Jaw—16-Sec.
Diner........★Enderlin and Portal.
Buffet Parlor..★North Portal and Moose Jaw.

No. 11—KOOTENAY EXPRESS—Medicine Hat to Vancouver.

Sleeper......★Calgary to Vancouver—12-Sec., D.R. (in No. 542 Calgary
    to MacLeod). ★Lethbridge to Nelson—12-Sec., D.R.
Cafe Parlor..★Calgary to Vancouver (in No. 542 Calgary to MacLeod).

No. 12—KETTLE VALLEY EXPRESS.
Vancouver to Medicine Hat.

Sleeper......★Vancouver to Calgary—12-Sec., D.R. (in No. 541 MacLeod
    to Calgary).
    ★Nelson to Lethbridge—12-Sec., D.R.
    ★Vancouver to Penticton—8-Sec., D.R., 2 Cpts. (Open
    until 8.00 a.m.)
Cafe Parlor...★Vancouver to Calgary (in No. 541 MacLeod to Calgary).

No. 17—Toronto to Sault Ste. Marie.

Sleeper......★Toronto to Sault Ste. Marie—8-Sec., D.R., 2 Cpt.
Cafe Parlor..★Sudbury to Sault Ste. Marie.

Montreal and Ottawa to Chicago, via Detroit and N. Y. C. 39.
On No. 15, a Pool Train, Montreal, Windsor Station, to Toronto.

Diner........★Montreal to Toronto. ★Detroit to Chicago.
Parlors ......★Montreal to Toronto.
Parlors.......★Ottawa to Toronto (in Pool 559, Ottawa-Brockville).
Sleepers......★Toronto to Chicago—12-Sec., D.R., 10 Rmtte., 6 D.B.R.
    ★Toronto to Detroit—8-Sec., 4 D. B. R. (Saturday). (May
    be occupied to 7.30 a.m. E. S. T., Sundays.)

No. 20—THE CANADIAN.
Chicago to Montreal, via N. Y. C. 358 and Detroit.
On No. 14, a Pool Train, Toronto to Montreal, Central Station.

Buffet.........Chicago to Detroit—6 D. B. R., Buffet Lounge.
Diner.........★Toronto to Montreal.
Parlor Cars..★Toronto to Montreal.
Cafe Parlor...★London to Toronto.
Sleepers.....★Chicago to Toronto—10 Rmtte., 6 D.B.R. and 12-Sec.,D.R.
    ★Detroit to Toronto—8-Sec., 4D.B.R. (Open 10.00 p.m.)

No. 21—CHICAGO EXPRESS.
Montreal to Chicago, via Detroit and N. Y. C. 31.
On No. 21, a Pool Train, Montreal, Windsor Station, to Toronto

Parlor........★Toronto to Detroit. ★Detroit to Chicago.
Diner.........★Toronto to Windsor. ★Detroit to Chicago.
Sleepers......★Montreal to Toronto—10 Cpt. (except Saturday). 12-Sec.,
    D.R., 14 S.B.R., 14 S.B.R. (except Saturday). 10 Room-
    ettes, 5 D.B.R., 1 D.R., 4 Cpt. (except Saturday).
Sleepers   ★Montreal to Hamilton—1 D. R., 4 Cpt. (except Satur-
open   day). (In 721, Toronto to Hamilton).
10.00 p.m. ★Montreal to London—8-Sec., D.R., 2 Cpts. (except Sat.).
    ★Montreal to Detroit—12-Sec., D.R. (except Saturday).
Buffet Sleepers..★Montreal to Hamilton—1 D.R., 4 Cpts. (in 721,
    Toronto to Hamilton). (Buffet open Montreal to Toronto.)
    ★Montreal to Toronto—1 D.R., 4 Cpt. (except Saturday).

No. 22—THE OVERSEAS.
Chicago to Montreal, via N. Y. C. 376 and Detroit.
On No. 22, a Pool Train, Toronto to Montreal, Windsor Station.

Diner........★Chicago to Detroit. ★Windsor to Toronto.
Parlor ....★Chicago to Detroit. ★Detroit to Toronto.
Sleepers......★Detroit to Montreal—10 Roomettes, 5 D.B.R.
(Sleepers ★London to Montreal—8-Sec., D.R., 2 Cpt. (except Sat.).
Toronto   ★Hamilton to Montreal—8-Sec., 4 D.B.R. (except Sat.).
open   (In No. 762, Hamilton to Toronto.) (Open 9.00 p.m.)
10.00 p.m.) ★Toronto to Montreal—10 Cpt. (except Saturday). 12-Sec.,
    D.R., 14 S.B.R., 14 S.B.R. (except Saturday).
Buffet Sleeper..★Hamilton to Montreal—1 D. R., 4 Cpts. (in 762,
    Hamilton to Toronto). (Buffet open Toronto to Montreal.)
    ★Toronto to Montreal—1 D.R., 4 Cpts. (except Saturday).

POOL 23 and 24—Ottawa and Toronto (via Belleville).

Sleepers.....★Ottawa and Toronto—14 S.B.R., 12-Sec., D.R. (2 Cars).
Buffet Sleeper..★Toronto to Ottawa—1 D.R., 4 Cpt.
    (Sleepers open Ottawa 10.00 p.m. and Toronto 10.00 p.m.)

No. 27—TORONTO TO SUDBURY.

Sleepers......★Toronto to Sudbury—12-Sec., D.R., 8-Sec., D.R. 2 Cpt.
    (except Saturday) 10 Roomettes, 5 D.B.R. (Handled
    in Train 3 on Sundays.)
Sleepers open 10.00 p.m.

No. 28—SAULT STE. MARIE-SUDBURY-TORONTO.

Cafe Parlor..★Sault Ste. Marie, Ont., to Sudbury.
Sleepers .....★Sudbury to Toronto—12-Sec., D.R., 8-Sec., D.R., 2 Cpt.
    (except Saturday) 10 Roomettes, 5 D.B.R.
    ★Sault Ste. Marie, Ont., to Toronto — 8-Sec., D.R., 2-Cpt.
    (Handled in Train 6, Sudbury to Toronto.)
(Sleepers Sudbury open 9.00 p.m. and to 8.00 a.m.)

POOL 33—Ottawa to Toronto, via Peterboro.

Sleepers ......Ottawa to Toronto. Open 10.00 p.m.
    ★12-Sec., D.R. (2 cars). ★8-Sec., D.R., 2-Cpt. ★14 S. B. R.

POOL 34—Toronto to Ottawa, via Peterboro.

Sleepers.......Toronto to Ottawa. Open 10.00 p.m.
    ★12-Sec., D.R. (2 cars.) ★14 S. B. R.
    ★8 Sec., D.R., 2 Cpt. (Saturday only.)

★—Regularly assigned cars Air-Conditioned.

---

automobiles did not present the kind of competition to rail transportation in Canada that they did in the United States, except for the urbanized eastern corridor between Quebec and Toronto, and in the metropolitan areas around western cities, such as Vancouver.

After a decade of relying on existing service, Canadian National launched a whole portfolio of new trains between 1954 and 1956. These included the Toronto to Algonquin Park *Algonquin*, the Edmonton to Halifax *Bluenose*, the new Montreal to Toronto *Lakeshore Express* and the ambitious and aptly named *Overlander*, which traveled the entire

length of Canada, from Halifax, Nova Scotia, to Vancouver, British Columbia, making it a true coast-to-coast service!

Nearly ten years later, between 1964 and 1966, even as ridership began to seriously dwindle, Canadian National ironically inaugurated another large selection of trains that we still recall as colorful, but which never really had a chance to become true classics. On 14 June 1964, on the fortieth anniversary of the great *Montrealer*, the *Chaleur* began running from Montreal to Campbellton, New Brunswick, and the *Champlain* initiated service between Montreal and Quebec. The date 31 October 1965 will always be remembered as the birthdate of more new Canadian trains than any other. Those—mostly short runs—that started to roll on that date include the Toronto to Sarnia *Metroliner*, the Montreal to Toronto *Bonaventure*, *Premier*, *Lakeshore* and *Rapido*, as well as the Montreal to Ottawa *Bytowner*, *Gatineau* and *Laurier*.

Joining these trains over the next two years were the Toronto to Windsor *Tecumseh*, the London to Toronto *Ontarian*, the Toronto to Sarnia *Huron* and the Toronto to Windsor *Erie*, which was named for the lake that passengers could see from their coach windows.

Among the last great passenger trains introduced by Canadian National were the *Expoliner*, which was put on the Belleville to Montreal run in 1967 during the Expo '67 World's Fair, and the Montreal to Toronto *Turbo*, which was added on 12 December 1968. The last notable train added to Canadian National's roster was the *Capitale*, which went into service between Brockville and Toronto on 25 April 1976.

By the 1970s, as with American rail passenger lines, both the Canadian National and the Canadian Pacific were forced to relinquish their badly slumping passenger business to unified government operation. In 1978, VIA Rail, Canada's equivalent to America's Amtrak, merged the passenger service of the two railways. Canadian National's passenger equipment was taken over on 31 March 1978 and VIA became a Crown Corporation the next day, although most of Canadian Pacific's passenger service had been acquired in September 1973. Most Canadian National and Canadian Pacific personnel involved in passenger service became employees of VIA. In September 1978, the two major transcontinental trains in Canada, Canadian National's *Super Continental* and Canadian Pacific's *Canadian*, were combined east of Winnipeg as the *Canadian*. More train combinations and discontinuations followed.

Although VIA may have served to preserve passenger service in Canada, many of the classic Canadian trains were discontinued, changed or merged. Notable among these was Canadian National's Montreal to Halifax *Scotian*. It was replaced by an extension of Canadian Pacific's Montreal to St John *Atlantic Limited* to Halifax. The *Atlantic*'s route through northern Maine provided a faster route, which became much more popular and heavily traveled than the older Canadian Pacific route.

A decade later during 1988, VIA Rail undertook a complete renovating program for all of its passenger stock. In the case of the *Canadian*, this meant a total restoration to the 1950s passenger car ambience. The original aura of these cars was brought into fresh prominence, and even more important, all heating and air conditioning systems were completely replaced with more modern equipment.

Today, the *Canadian* is no longer a daily service, but does operate three days a week between Toronto and Vancouver, via Winnipeg, Saskatoon, Edmonton and Jasper. It provides coach and sleeping car accommodations and features lounges, meal service facilities and dome cars. Connecting service is also provided three days a week between Jasper, Prince George and Prince Rupert by the *Skeena*, with coach, meal service and sleeping car facilities available.

The *Canadian*'s route still includes historic cities and magnificent scenery. Toronto, the capital of the Province of Ontario, is the starting point for the current itinerary. After traversing the Canadian Great Lakes region, the *Canadian* crosses the vast expanse of the Canadian Shield, a region that was thoroughly sculpted by Ice Age glaciers. Here, sparkling lakes punctuate a beautiful, pristine forest land. From there, the *Canadian* moves onto Hornepayne, then Armstrong, and finally, Winnipeg, Manitoba's capital and Canada's oldest western city. From Winnipeg, the *Canadian* follows the second leg of the old *Super Continental* route to Vancouver via Saskatoon, Edmonton and Jasper. The Rockies are increasingly in evidence as the train nears Jasper. Jasper is surrounded by mountains, and lakes and snowcapped peaks are in abundance. Between Red Pass and Jackman, Mount Robson—also called 'The Dome'—rises into the clouds, to the north. At 12,972 feet, this is the highest peak in the Canadian Rockies.

Emerald green lakes, spectacular waterfalls, spruce, pine and fir forests and fields of mountain wildflowers provide extraordinary vistas for this part of the *Canadian*'s itinerary. On the last leg of its journey, the *Canadian* passes through rolling, rugged, dusty hills and canyons, accented here and there by a patch of vegetation where irrigation has been successful. The train then follows the

Below: The Canadian National's classic *Ocean Limited* glides across the sturdy trestle at Belaeil, Quebec, circa 1954.

powerful Fraser River through its spectacular steep canyon. Even as the westbound *Canadian* is coming into the Main Street Station, Vancouver on the fifth day of travel, an eastbound train is being prepared for that evening's trip to Toronto.

Meanwhile, VIA Rail links the Atlantic coast of Canada to central Canada through two full-service trains—the *Atlantic* and the *Ocean.* The former is a descendant of the old Winnipeg to Quebec train of the same name, while the *Ocean* traces its heritage to the classic *Ocean Limited* service between Montreal and Halifax that first ran in 1904.

Both trains provide coach and sleeping car accommodations and feature a lounge, meal service facilities and dome cars.

The *Ocean* provides service three days a week between Halifax and Montreal via Campbellton and Mont-Joli. Six-day-a-week service is available between Halifax and Moncton.

The *Chaleur* operates three days a week between Gaspe and Montreal with coach and sleeping car accommodations, a lounge and meal facilities, and service is now offered between Matapedia and Montreal six days a week.

Left: Passengers of today aboard VIA Rail Canada's *Ocean*, the successor to the Canadian National's *Ocean Limited*.

THE GREAT TRUNK LINES

Below and opposite: The Pennsylvania Railroad's *Broadway Limited* was the epitome of the classic trunk line streamliner from the golden age of rail travel, while the Pennsylvania Railroad itself promoted itself as a powerful and dependable friend of travellers.

Of the great trunk lines, the largest in terms of the number of people it carried in its passenger trains was the Pennsylvania, and on the Pennsylvania Railroad, no other streamliner captured the same magic and excitement as the *Broadway Limited*, which ran between Chicago and New York.

The *Broadway Limited* was 25 tons of locomotive and 35,000 gallons of water pulling individual cars with names such as *Herald Square*, *Craigie House* and *James Whitcomb Riley*. Passengers would leave Chicago in the afternoon, go to bed at Fort Wayne, Indiana, and fall asleep at the legendary Horseshoe Curve in Pennsylvania. If one was awake, one would see the *Broadway Limited* pull into Altoona at 3:00 am, where locomotives were standing in sociable groups in the dark, with white plumes of steam rising into the stillness. On the next track would be a long string of silent cars, the maroon and gold of the Pennsylvania Railroad, and a switchman standing watchful with a lantern at the tail end, faithful as Orion. By the start of the business day, passengers stepped out of the grandly baroque Pennsylvania Station on New York's Seventh Avenue, ready for the day ahead. The *Broadway Limited* also had memorable sister trains on the 'Pennsy' between New York and Chicago, but none so glorious as she. Among these ladies were the *Pennsylva-*

Broadway Limited

The finest way to go between

NEW YORK • PHILADELPHIA • CHICAGO

You take more than a trip when you travel on this superb train. You're as comfortable as in the finest air-conditioned hotel. Privacy is complete in the attractively furnished room of your choice —*there are six types* on the Broadway ! Two beautiful lounge cars invite you to roam and relax. And the savory dishes concocted by master chefs are traditional treats in themselves. You'll love the Broadway—*and there's no extra fare!*

RAIN OR SHINE

Serving the Nation

...this great ALL-WEATHER FLEET goes through on time!

Spring weather can be mighty uncertain. But there's nothing uncertain about Pennsylvania Railroad's great East-West Fleet! These fine modern trains always go ...always get you there—365 days a year.

And in what elegance and comfort you ride! In Pullman Lounges richly endowed with the smartest appointments — soft divans, easy chairs, murals, mirrors, radio, beverage bars. Even the Diners are like gay cafes! And you retire to real beds in the privacy of Roomettes, Duplex Rooms, Bedrooms, Compartments, Drawing Rooms, Master Rooms—or to modern Section Sleepers.

If you go "Coach", enjoy restful reclining seats. The cost? Pullman or Coach, *very little*, because FARES ARE LOW. So why chance the whim of weather . . . when this great East-West Fleet is better for you . . . *all ways . . . all the time!*

17 TRAINS DAILY...
between New York, Philadelphia and Chicago

7 TRAINS DAILY...
between New York, Philadelphia and St. Louis Washington, Baltimore and St. Louis

10 TRAINS DAILY...
between Washington, Baltimore and Chicago

40 TRAINS DAILY...
between New York and Washington

Plus a fleet daily serving Pittsburgh, Columbus, Cincinnati, Akron, Cleveland, Detroit, Dayton, Louisville

GO NOW—PAY LATER. Ask about Travel-Credit Plan.

A Grand Outlook is yours from the richly appointed solarium of Pullman Observation Cars.

ENJOY THE TRAIL BLAZER
de luxe all-coach train NEW YORK-CHICAGO..17 hours
Observation Car...Radio...Club Lounge...low priced meals...Reserved individual reclining seat at no extra cost . . . attendants—all at low fares! Reclining-seat coaches on The Trail Blazer between Washington and Chicago, too; and on other trains to many cities.
COMING — NEW ALL-COACH TRAIN BETWEEN NEW YORK AND ST. LOUIS!

THE SHORTEST ROUTE BETWEEN EAST AND WEST Serves America's largest cities. Through cars to New England and the South. Convenient connections to the West.

Everything at your command—real bed, individual toilet facilities, wardrobe—in the thrifty Roomette.

Pennsylvania Railroad

nia Limited, the *Manhattan Limited* and the *Gotham Limited.*

The *Liberty Limited* ran between Chicago and Washington, while the *Patriot* was an appropriately named streamliner that had as its main route the main street of early American history. Operated jointly by the Pennsylvania Railroad and the New York, New Haven & Hartford, the *Patriot* ran from Washington, DC, to Boston via New York. The *Jeffersonian,* named for an unparalleled patriot, linked New York and St Louis.

The Pennsylvania Railroad launched its *Washingtonian,* which ran via the New Haven, Boston & Maine and Canadian National from Philadelphia to Montreal. Other Pennsylvania trains included the *Congressional,* the *Constitution,* the *Executive,* the *President,* the *Federal,* the *Judiciary,* the *Embassy,* the *Legislator* and the *Senator.* It might be noted that the Southern Pacific also had a *Senator* which operated between Sacramento and San Francisco. *The Representative,* the *Statesman* the *Speaker,* the *Admiral,* the *Commander,* and perhaps the *Mount Vernon, Arlington* and *Potomac* were included, and on a state level, there was the *Governor,* which ran from Philadelphia to Harrisburg.

Like the *Patriot,* the *Senator* was also operated jointly by the Pennsylvania Railroad and the New York, New Haven & Hartford. One can almost picture the faces that would have been present for power lunches in the club car of this renowned streamliner that once plied

the tracks between Washington, DC, and Boston via New York City. In 1881, the Pennsylvania Railroad launched what is said to have been the first extra-fare train in history. Originally called the *New York-Chicago Limited,* it was rechristened the *Pennsylvania Limited* in 1891. In the beginning, the train was all-Pullman—an innovation—as well as being gas-lighted, but passengers still had to use a hand-pump to draw water in the lavatory. Dining cars were added a year later, electric lights in 1887 and an observation car in 1889.

In that same year the Pennsylvania Railroad inaugurated the *Pennsylvania Special* (not to be confused with the later *Pennsylvania Limited*), which ten years later began challenging the *Twentieth Century* as the renamed *Broadway Limited.* Attempting schedules practically impossible to maintain, the two competing roads reduced them by mutual agreement for a few years after 1912 until improved equipment made the previously advertised greater speeds practical. One of the Pennsylvania Railroad's archetypal streamliners, the *South Wind* linked Chicago with Miami.

The Pennsylvania Railroad was early in seizing upon the names of revolutionary patriots and signers of the Declaration of Independence for parlor cars on its *Congressional Limited-Gouverneur* (sic). These included *Benjamin Franklin, Thomas Jefferson, Caesar Rodney, Charles Carroll, Richard Henry Lee, Roger Sherman* and *John Hancock.* The

Below: During the 1930s, and well beyond, the Pennsylvania Railroad's classic *Washingtonian* was pulled by a powerful Baldwin-General Electric GG1.

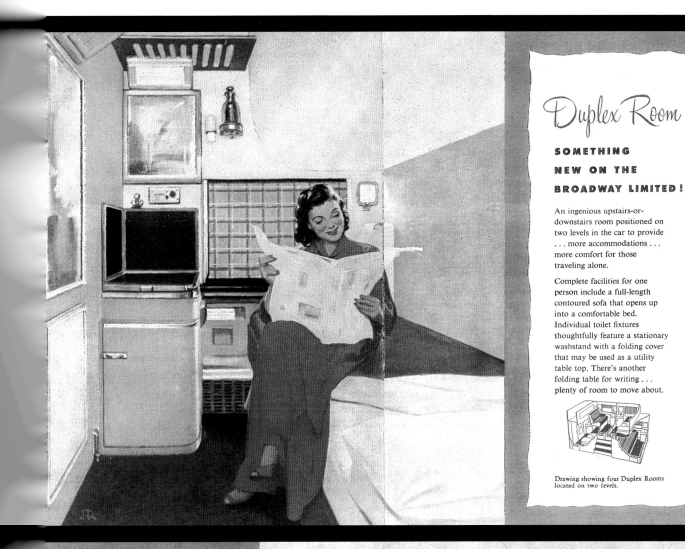

Duplex Room

SOMETHING NEW ON THE BROADWAY LIMITED!

An ingenious upstairs-or-downstairs room positioned on two levels in the car to provide . . . more accommodations . . . more comfort for those traveling alone.

Complete facilities for one person include a full-length contoured sofa that opens up into a comfortable bed. Individual toilet fixtures thoughtfully feature a stationary washstand with a folding cover that may be used as a utility table top. There's another folding table for writing . . . plenty of room to move about.

Drawing showing four Duplex Rooms located on two levels.

SO INVITING—
THE Master Dining Car

You'll detect it the moment you enter . . . sense its significance when the steward greets you. New beauty . . . new spaciousness . . . the *Broadway Limited's* traditional high standard of courteous, meticulous service . . . the festive experience of dining out and the anticipation of delicious food—served you by carefully trained personnel. Pastel-shaded linens, gleaming silverware, the soft harmony of color and charm, the diversified menu—*there's a new treat in dining awaiting you here!*

Fine foods are prepared in the *Broadway Limited's* modern stainless steel kitchen—located in an adjoining car.

PENNSYLVANIA RAILROAD
Serving the Nation

THROUGH CAR SERVICE—WESTWARD

Abbreviations: C.—Compartment; D. R.—Drawing-room; S.—Sections.
Coaches on all trains except Nos. 29 and 31.
Regularly assigned cars are Air-Conditioned.

No. 1—PENNSYLVANIA LIMITED. (Tables 1, 13.)
Lounge Car....New York to Chicago—(6 Double Bedrooms, Bar).
Sleeping Cars..New York to San Francisco—(10 Roomettes, 6 Double Bedrooms). (April 1 and every other day thereafter.) (To C. B. & Q. No. 17.)
New York to San Francisco—(10 Roomettes, 6 Double Bedrooms). (April 2 and every other day thereafter.) (To C. & N. W. No. 27.)
New York to Chicago—(21 Roomettes).
New York to Chicago—(6 S., 6 Double Bedrooms).
New York to Chicago—(12 S., D.R.) (Two Cars.)
Washington to Chicago—(8 S., 2 C., D.R.).
Dining Cars....New York to Chicago. Washington to Harrisburg.
Coaches ......New York to Chicago—(Reclining Seats).
Washington to Harrisburg.

No. 3—THE PENN TEXAS. (Tables 5, 13.)
Sleeping Cars..New York to El Paso—(14 Roomettes, 4 Dble. Bedrooms). (To Mo. Pac. No. 1.)
New York to Houston—(10 Roomettes, 6 Double Bedrooms). (To Mo. Pac. No. 21.)
New York to San Antonio—(10 Roomettes, 6 Double Bedrooms). (To Mo. Pac. No. 21.)
New York to San Antonio—14 Roomettes, 4 Double Bedrooms) or (10 Roomettes, 6 Double Bedrooms). (To Frisco-Katy No. 1.)
New York to St. Louis—(10 Roomettes, 5 Dble. Bdrms.).
New York to St. Louis—(12 S., D.R.).
New York to Columbus — (12 Duplex Rooms, 4 Double Bedrooms). (Daily, except Saturday.)
Washington to St. Louis-Houston — (10 Roomettes, 6 Double Bedrooms.) (To Mo. Pac. No. 21.)
Parlor Cafe Car..Indianapolis to Louisville. (In No. 326.)
Dining Cars....New York to St. Louis.
St. Louis to Dallas-Fort Worth. (In Mo. Pac. No. 1.)
St. Louis to San Antonio-Houston—(Lounge). (In Mo. Pac. No. 21.)
St. Louis to Springfield, Muskogee to San Antonio. (In Frisco-Katy No. 1.)
Fort Worth to El Paso—(Lounge). (In T. & P. No. 1.)
Recreation Car..New York to St. Louis. (Bar.) (For Pullman and Coach passengers.)
Coaches........New York to St. Louis—(Reclining Seats).
Washington to Harrisburg—(Reclining Seats).
St. Louis to El Paso—(Reclining Seats). (In Mo. Pac. 1.)
St. Louis to Houston—(Reclining Seats). (In Mo. Pac. 21.)
St. Louis to San Antonio—(Reclining Seats). (In Mo. Pac. No. 21.)
St. Louis to San Antonio—(Reclining Seats). (In Frisco-Katy No. 1.)

Nos. 13 and 13-85—MAIL and EXPRESS. (Table 13.)
Coaches ....New York to Pittsburgh—(Reclining Seats).

No. 23—MANHATTAN LIMITED. (Tables 1, 13.)
Lounge Car....New York to Chicago—(3 Double Bedrooms, D.R., Bar).
Sleeping Cars..New York to Chicago—(10 Roomettes, 5 Dble. Bdrms.).
New York to Chicago—(12 S., D.R.).
Washington to Chicago—(8 S., 2 C., D.R.) (Saturday) (from No. 33 arriving Pittsburgh 9 10 p.m.)
Pittsburgh to Chicago—(21 Roomettes) and (12 Duplex Rooms, 4 Double Bedrooms). (Two Cars.) (Saturday.) (Open 9 30 p.m.)
Sleeping cars may be occupied in Chicago until 7 50 a.m.
Dining Car......New York to Chicago.
Coaches........New York to Chicago—(Reclining Seats).

Nos. 25 and 25-329—THE METROPOLITAN. (Tables 6, 13.)
Parlor Cars.....New York to Pittsburgh.
Pittsburgh to Cleveland—(Buffet). (Via Youngstown.) (In No. 329.)
Dining Car......New York to Pittsburgh.
Coaches........New York to Pittsburgh—(Reclining Seats).
Pittsburgh to Cleveland. (Via Youngstown.) (In No. 329.)

NO. 29—BROADWAY LIMITED. (Tables 1, 13.)
Lounge Car....New York to Chicago—(2 Double Bedrooms, Bar).
Sleeping Cars..New York to Los Angeles—(4 C., 2 D.R., 4 Dble. Bdrms.). (To Santa Fe No. 19, Extra Fare west of Chicago.)
New York to Chicago—(21 Roomettes).
New York to Chicago — (4 C., 2 D.R., 4 Double Bedrooms). (Two Cars.)
New York to Chicago—(10-Roomettes, 6 Double Bedrooms). (Four Cars.)
New York to Chicago—(12 Duplex Rooms, 4 Dble. Bdrms.).
Observation Car..New York to Chicago—(2 Master Rooms, Double Bedroom, Bar Lounge).
Dining Car......New York to Chicago. No Coaches or checked baggage.

No. 31—"SPIRIT OF ST. LOUIS." (Tables 5, 13.)
Lounge Car....New York to St. Louis—(6 Double Bedrooms, Bar).
Sleeping Cars..New York to St. Louis—(14 S.).
New York to St. Louis—(21 Roomettes).
New York to St. Louis—(4 C., 2 D.R., 4 Dbl. Bedrooms).
New York to St. Louis—(12 Duplex Rooms, 4 Double Bedrooms).
New York to Indianapolis—(10 Roomettes, 6 Dble. Bdrms.).
New York to Indianapolis—(21 Roomettes).
Washington to St. Louis—(14 S.).
Washington to St. Louis—(10 Roomettes, 6 Dbl. Bdrms.).
Washington to Indianapolis — (10 Roomettes, 5 Double Bedrooms). (Daily, except Saturday.)
Observation Car..Washington to St. Louis—(C., 2 D.R., Double Bedroom, Bar).
Dining Cars....New York to St. Louis.
Washington to Harrisburg.
No Coaches or checked baggage.

Nos. 33, 33-105 and 33-203. THE ST. LOUISAN. (Tables 5, 6, 7, 13.)
Lounge Car....New York to St. Louis—(6 Double Bedrooms, Bar).
Sleeping Cars..New York to St. Louis—(21 Roomettes).
New York to St. Louis—(6 S., 6 Double Bedrooms).
New York to Louisville—(6 S., 6 Double Bedrooms). (To 326 at Indianapolis.) (Open Indianapolis to 5 30 a.m.)
Washington to St. Louis—(12 S., D.R.).
Pittsburgh to New Orleans—(10 S., 2 Double Bedrooms, 1 D.R.). (In No. 203 via Cincinnati and L. & N. R.R.) (Open 10 00 p.m.)
Pittsburgh to Cincinnati—(18 Roomettes). (In No. 203.) (Open 10 00 p.m.) (May be occupied until 7 30 a.m.)
Pittsburgh to Columbus—(12 S., D. R.). (Daily, except Saturday.) (In No. 203.) (Open 10 00 p.m.) (May be occupied until 8 00 a.m.)
Pittsburgh to Detroit—(6 S., 6 Dble. Bdrms.). (Open 10 00 p.m.) (In No. 105.)
Pittsburgh to Detroit—(10 Roomettes, 5 Double Bedrooms). (Daily, except Saturday.) (Open 10 00 p.m.) (In No. 105.)
Parlor Cafe Car..Indianapolis to Louisville. (In No. 326.)
Dining Car......New York to St. Louis.
Coaches........New York to St. Louis—(Reclining Seats).
Washington to Pittsburgh—(Reclining Seats).
Pittsburgh to Cincinnati—(Reclining Seats). (In No. 203.)
Pittsburgh to Detroit—(Reclining Seats). (In No. 105.)

No. 33-63—THE ST. LOUISAN AND THE GOLDEN TRIANGLE. (Table 1.)
(Daily, except Saturday.)
Lounge Car....Pittsburgh to Chicago—(3 Double Bdrms., D.R., Buffet).
Sleeping Cars..Washington to Chicago—(8 S., 2 C., D.R.).
Pittsburgh to Chicago—(10 Roomettes, 6 Double Bdrms.).
Pittsburgh to Chicago—(12 Duplex Rooms, 5 Dble. Bdrms.).
Pittsburgh to Chicago—(12 S., D.R.).
Pittsburgh to Chicago—(4 C., 2 D.R., 4 Dbl. Bdrms.).
Pittsburgh to Chicago — (12 Duplex Rooms, 4 Double Bedrooms).
Pittsburgh to Chicago— (21 Roomettes).
(Sleeping cars open in Pittsburgh 9 30 p.m.; occupied until 7 35 a.m.)
Dining Car.....Harrisburg to Pittsburgh.
Coaches........Washington to Pittsburgh—(Reclining Seats).
Pittsburgh to Chicago—(Reclining Seats).
No checked baggage Pittsburgh to Chicago. (In No. 63.)

Nos. 35 and 35-363—PITTSBURGH NIGHT EXPRESS. (Tables 6, 13.)
(Daily, except Saturday nights.)
Lounge Car....Philadelphia to Pittsburgh—(6 Single Bedrooms, Buffet).
Sleeping Cars..Philadelphia to Pittsburgh—(12 Duplex Rooms, 5 Double Bedrooms).
Philadelphia to Pittsburgh—(12 S., D.R.).
Philadelphia to Pittsburgh—(21 Roomettes).
(Sleeping cars open in Broad Street Station 10 00 p.m., may be occupied in Pittsburgh until 8 00 a.m.)
Parlor Car.....Pittsburgh to Cleveland. (Via Salem.) (In No. 363.)
Dining Car.....Pittsburgh to Cleveland—(Lounge). (Via Salem.) (In No. 363.)
Coaches........Philadelphia to Pittsburgh—(Reclining Seats).
Pittsburgh to Cleveland. (Via Salem.) (In No. 363.)

No. 35-37—PITTSBURGH NIGHT EXPRESS. (Table 13.)
(Daily, except Saturday nights.)
Sleeping Car...Philadelphia to Pittsburgh—(8 S., 2 C., D.R.). (Open in Broad Street Station 10 00 p.m.)

Alexander Hamilton had a distinctive design of 12 parlor seats, 16 lounge seats, eight sun room seats and one drawing room and buffet. Meanwhile, hundreds of other cars of all types were named for notables and near-notables in every type of political, military, social, professional, industrial, railroad and business sector in America.

These were the *Roger Williams, Thomas Paine, Thomas Hart Benton, Daniel Boone, Salmon P Chase, John Hunt Morgan, Joel Chandler Harris, George Westinghouse, Walter Reed, James D Eads, Roger B Taney, Admiral Dewey, Samuel Morse, Cyrus HK Curtis* and *Cyrus H McCormick*. There was also a *Samuel Adams*, predating Jim Koch's popular brand of beer by nearly a century. It was *not* a club car. The Pennsylvania also used names of its own past corporate presidents, including *William Chamberlain Patterson, Alexander Johnston Cassatt* and *William Wallace Atterbury*. These were painted along the sides of the cars in full without a thought of even condensing the lettering!

The Pennsylvania's New York to Washington *Edison* took notice of the fact that it passed through Menlo Park, where the great inventor's famous early workshop was located. The Pennsylvania Railroad also named a train for *Nellie Bly*, the famous globetrotter. Nellie Bly was, of course, the pen name of Elizabeth Cochrane Seaman, who lived from 1866 to 1922 and captured the public's imagination and won eternal fame for accepting the challenge of Jules Verne's *Around the World in 80 Days* by circumnavigating the globe in 72 days, six hours and 11 minutes.

When the Pennsylvania Railroad's *Pennsylvania Limited* on the New York to

Chicago run became the first all-Pullman train in 1887, it strove for global implications with its specially built sleepers named *Germany, England, France, Italy, China* and *Spain*. There were not, however, dining cars called *Greece* and *Turkey*, as was erroneously mentioned in Carlson Bennet's satirical 1902 poem. The Pennsylvania continued to use place names until its supply began to run low, as proven when it christened a sleeper *Gap*, for a little town on its main line.

Indeed, the Pennsylvania acquired more of a sense of humor in its old age. In the summer of 1953, it announced a freight train serving the Southwest, to be known as the *Texas-Oklahoma-Missouri-Kansas-Arkansas-Traveler*, or simply *TOMKAT*. They most certainly must have known that the Norfolk & Western also had a *Tom Cat*, too, properly spelled, as well as a *Catbird*.

On a more serious note, the competition between the Pennsylvania Railroad's *Broadway Limited* and the New York Central's *Twentieth Century Limited* became the most celebrated rivalry in the history of North American railroads. They kept pace with each other in service, speed and luxury, with the major difference lying in the nature of the two routes. The *Broadway*'s route was more direct, but went through some fairly mountainous terrain. The New York Central's route formed a 90-degree angle—due north to Albany, then due west to Chicago. The main line traveled through the relatively flat terrain of the Hudson and Mohawk Valleys and the Great Lakes shore, a situation that fostered use of the term 'Water Level Route' in New York Central's advertising. The implication was that the level route would provide passengers with a more comfortable ride and a better night's sleep. Today's *Broadway Limited*, operated by Amtrak, completes its 911-mile run from New York to Chicago in 18 hours, albeit clearing Altoona at a more convenient hour both ways.

George Daniels, the fabled New York Central passenger agent, a short, plump man sporting a white goatee, bombarded the management with ideas from the moment he was hired. Daniels convinced the New York Central's managers to run a special New York to Buffalo train called the *Empire State Express*. A special big-wheeled, Atlantic-type locomotive was constructed just to haul the train. On 14 September 1891, the 436-mile run

from New York to Buffalo was made in seven hours and six minutes, including stops, at an average speed of 61.4 mph, a new record.

George Daniels wanted to run the fastest, most luxurious train in the country on the New York to Chicago route. He could have continued to call the train the *Empire State Express*, but he wanted a new name to evoke the idea of continuing progress into the new century, so he chose to call it the *Twentieth Century*. Shortly thereafter, when it was decided to limit the number of stops, the name was altered to the *Twentieth Century Limited*. Service on the new train started in 1902, and was scheduled to make the

Opposite: **Powered by the big GG1 electrics, the Pennsylvania Railroad's service between New York's Pennsylvania Station and the nation's capital included the classic *Senator*, as well as both a *Morning* and *Afternoon Congressional*. Advertising material boasted that these were 'America's most beautiful daylight trains.'**

NEW YORK CENTRAL SYSTEM
The Water Level Route—You Can Sleep

PULLMAN, COACH AND DINING CAR SERVICE EASTBOUND
Regularly assigned cars are air-conditioned.
Air-conditioned equipment is assigned as far as possible but the right is reserved to employ non air-conditioned cars as necessitated by volume of traffic or emergencies.

No. 2—The Pacemaker—Daily—Streamliner.
All seats reserved.
Observation Lounge Coach..Chicago to New York.
Lounge Coach..Chicago to New York.
Dining Service.
Reclining Seat Coaches..Chicago to New York.

No. 4—The James Whitcomb Riley—Daily—Streamliner.
All seats reserved.
Observation Lounge Coach..Chicago to Cincinnati.
Reclining Seat Coaches..Chicago to Cincinnati.
Dining Service.

No. 6—Fifth Avenue Special—Daily.
Lounge Sleeping Car..Chicago to New York—8-Section—Buffet.
  Niagara Falls to New York—6 Double Bedroom, Buffet (from No. 246 at Buffalo).
Sleeping Cars— *Open at Rochester* 9 00 *p.m.*
  Chicago to New York—10 Roomette, 5 Double Bedroom.
  Chicago to New York—14 Section.
  Cleveland to New York—10 Roomette, 6 Dble. Bedroom.
  Niagara Falls to New York—17 Roomette (from No. 246 at Buffalo).
  Rochester to New York (except Saturday) — 13 Double Bedroom.
  Rochester to New York— 22 Roomette.
  Rochester to New York—8-Section, 5 Double Bedroom.
Dining Service..Chicago to Buffalo.
Parlor Car (N.Y.C. Car)..Chicago to Cleveland.
Tavern Lounge Coach..Chicago to Cleveland.
Coaches........Chicago to New York (Reclining Seat).

No. 8—The Wolverine—Daily.
Leaves from La Salle Street Station.
Lounge Sleeping Car..Chicago to New York—6 Dble. Bedroom—Buffet.
Sleeping Cars— *Open at Buffalo* 9 00 *p.m.*
  Chicago to New York—10 Roomette, 6 Double Bedroom.—(Two.)
  Chicago to New York—22 Roomette.
  Detroit to New York—10 Roomette, 6 Double Bedroom.
  Detroit to New York (Sat. only)—12 Double Bedroom.
  Detroit to New York (Saturday only)—22 Roomette.
  Buffalo to New York (except Saturday)—12-Section, Drawing-room.
Observation Parlor Car (N.Y.C. Car)..Chicago to Detroit.
Dining Service.
Tavern Lounge Coach..Chicago to Detroit.
Coaches........Chicago to New York (Reclining Seat).

No. 10—The Mohawk—Daily.
Sleeping Cars— *May be occupied until* 8 00 *a.m. at Buffalo.*
  Chicago to New York—10 Roomette, 6 Double Bedroom.
  Chicago to Buffalo (daily, except Saturday)—12-Section, Drawing-room.
  Cincinnati to Buffalo — 22 Roomette (from No. 424 at Cleveland.)
Dining Cars....Chicago to Toledo.
  Buffalo to Albany—Diner Lounge.
Coaches........Chicago to New York.

No. 12—Southwestern Limited—Daily.
Observation Lounge Sleeping Car..St. Louis to New York—5 Double Bedroom—Buffet.
Buffet breakfast service into New York.
Sleeping Cars..St. Louis to New York—10 Roomette, 6 Double Bedroom.—(Two.)
  St. Louis to New York—14-Section.
  St. Louis to Boston—10 Roomette, 6 Double Bedroom (in No. 78 from Cleveland).
  St. Louis to Boston—14-Section (in 78 from Cleveland).
  Cleveland to New York (Saturday only)—10 Roomette, 6 Double Bedroom.
From No. 382 at Buffalo.
  Toronto to New York—10 Roomette, 6 Dble. Bdrm. (3).
  Toronto to New York (except Saturday)—13 Double Bedroom.
  Toronto to New York—12-Section, Drawing-room.
Dining Car......St. Louis to Cleveland.
Coaches........St. Louis to New York (Reclining Seat).
  St. Louis to Boston (Reclining Seat) (in No. 78 from Cleveland).

No. 16—Ohio State Limited—Daily—Streamliner.
Observation Lounge Sleeping Car..Cincinnati to New York—5 Double Bedroom—Buffet.
Sleeping Cars..Cincinnati to New York—10 Roomette, 6 Dble. Bdrm. (3).
  Columbus to New York—10 Roomette, 6 Double Bedroom.
  Cincinnati to Boston—10 Roomette, 6 Double Bedroom (in No. 78 from Cleveland).
  Cleveland to New York (Saturday only)—10 Roomette, 6 Double Bedroom.
Lounge Coach..Cincinnati to New York.
Dining Service.
Coaches........Cincinnati to New York (Reclining Seat).

No. 22—Lake Shore Limited—Daily.
Lounge Sleeping Car..Chicago to New York—6 Double Bedroom—Buffet.
Sleeping Cars..Los Angeles to New York—10 Roomette, 6 Double Bedroom (from U. P.-C. & N. W. No. 2 at Chicago).
  San Francisco to New York—10 Roomette, 6 Double Bedroom (from S.P.-U.P.-C. & N. W. No. 28 at Chicago) (leaves San Francisco April 2, 4 and every other day thereafter).
  San Francisco to New York—10 Roomette, 6 Double Bedroom (from W. P.-D. & R. G. W.-C. B. & Q. No. 18 at Chicago—leaves San Francisco April 1, 3 and every other day thereafter).
  Chicago to New York—10 Roomette, 6 Double Bedroom.
  Chicago to New York (except Saturday)—10 Roomette, 5 Double Bedroom.
  Chicago to New York—22 Roomette.
  Chicago to New York—12-Section, Drawing-room.
  Chicago to Boston—10 Roomette, 5 Double Bedroom.
  Chicago to Boston—8-Sec., 4 Double Bedroom.
  Detroit to New York (daily, except Saturday)—12-Section, Drawing-room (from No. 364 at Buffalo).
  St. Louis to Boston—8-Section, 5 Double Bedroom (from No. 24 at Albany).
Dining Service.
Coaches........Chicago to New York (Reclining Seat).
  Utica to New York (from No. 138 at Albany).
  Albany to Boston.

No. 24—The Knickerbocker—Daily.
Lounge Sleeping Car..St. Louis to New York—6 Double Bedroom—Buffet.
Sleeping Cars— *Open at Cleveland* 9 30 *p.m.*
  St. Louis to New York—10 Roomette, 6 Double Bedroom.
  St. Louis to New York—12-Section, Drawing-room.
  St. Louis to Boston—8-Section, 5 Double Bedroom (in No. 22 from Albany).
  St. Louis to Richmond, Va. — 10 Roomette, 6 Double Bedroom (in No. 406 from Indianapolis—C.&O. No. 4-46 from Cincinnati).
  Cincinnati to New York — 22 Roomette (from No. 424 at Cleveland.)
  Cleveland to New York—10 Roomette, 6 Double Bedroom.
  Cleveland to Toronto—8-Section, 5 Double Bedroom (in No. 372 from Buffalo).
  Pittsburgh to Albany (except Saturday) — 10 Roomette, 5 Double Bedroom (from P. & L. E. No. 33—N. Y. C. No. 284 at Buffalo).
Dining Service.
Coaches........St. Louis to New York (Reclining Seat).
  St. Louis to Cincinnati (in No. 406 from Indianapolis).

No. 26—Twentieth Century Limited—Daily—Streamliner.
Special service charge.
Observation Lounge Sleeping Car..Chicago to New York — 5 Double Bedroom—Buffet.
Club Lounge Car (Buffet)..Chicago to New York.
Sleeping Cars..Los Angeles to New York — 4 Compartment, 4 Double Bedroom, 2 D.R. (from Santa Fe No. 20 at Chicago).
  Los Angeles to New York—10 Roomette, 6 Double Bedroom (from Santa Fe No. 20 at Chicago).
  Chicago to New York — 4 Compartment, 4 Double Bedroom, 2 Drawing-room. (Three.)
  Chicago to New York—12 Double Bedroom. (Three.)
  Chicago to New York—10 Rmtte., 6 Dble. Bdrm. (Two.)
Dining Service.
Pullman Cars only; no coach passengers carried.

No. 28—New England States—Daily—Streamliner.
Observation Lounge Sleeping Car..Chicago to Boston — 5 Double Bedroom—Buffet.
Sleeping Cars..Chicago to Boston—10 Roomette, 6 Double Bedroom. (Four.)
  Chicago to Boston—22 Roomette.
  Detroit to Boston (except Saturday)— 10 Roomette, 6 Double Bedroom (from No. 48 at Buffalo).
  Pittsburgh to Boston—10 Roomette, 6 Double Bedroom (from P. & L. E. No. 33—N.Y.C. No. 284 at Buffalo).
Dining Service.
Reclining Seat Coaches..Chicago to Boston—all seats reserved.
Lounge Coach..Chicago to Boston.

Easy Does It...when the family goes New York Central

Easy on Dad! No traffic to tire him. No white line to watch. When New York Central does the driving, he's free to read, nap, or enjoy the wonderful *Water Level Route* scenery that parades past his big picture window.

Easy on the Kids! They don't have to stay put in their seats. There's plenty of room to move about. And there's the extra thrill of those famous New York Central meals in the diner, with their own, thrifty Children's Menu to choose from.

Easy on Mother, because her mind's at ease about the youngsters. No back-seat fidgets. No frequent roadside stops. Everything the children need is right at hand. And they couldn't be safer at home!

Easy on the Budget! Round-trip coach fares are low. And special Family Tickets cut them as much as 50% or even more. Ask your New York Central ticket agent all about them.

New York Central

The Scenic Water Level Route

Above: **The Pennsylvania Railroad reached Chicago from New York by crossing the mountains. The rival New York Central expended much energy touting its 'Water Level Route.'**

Opposite: **Like the Pennsylvania Railroad's *Broadway Limited*, the rival New York Central *Twentieth Century Limited* was the epitome of the classic trunk line streamliners.**

960-mile run to Chicago in 20 hours, for an average speed of 80 mph.

Daniels planned the *Twentieth Century Limited* as a train for wealthy and important people who required speed, demanded luxury and could pay for both. The train was due to arrive in New York at 9:30 am, allowing businessmen a full day's work and pleasure travelers time for a taxi to the docks to board transatlantic liners. The train was all intended to be all-Pullman. This was contrary to past history when, because of their rivalry, the Vanderbilts had spurned Pullman cars and used Wagner Palace Car Company cars for the New York Central. By

the turn of the century, the Wagner Palace Car Company had been absorbed by Pullman. The use of his cars on the crack train of the railroad that had snubbed him for so many years must have been a source of gloating satisfaction to George Pullman.

Over the years, both the speed and the amenities of the *Twentieth Century Limited* were constantly improved. Passengers could sleep in their own roomettes and dine in the recently introduced dining car. They could avail themselves of a barber shop, a beauty salon, secretarial services, and telephone and telegraph facilities. The original train consisted of three sleepers, a diner and a library-buffet car. Later versions included cars with drawing rooms. The train became so popular that it was run in several sections, the wooden cars being replaced by all-steel equipment between 1910 and 1912. By the mid-1920s, the New York Central was calling the train a 'national institution,' and it had, in fact, become a source of patriotic pride. In 1912, the Pennsylvania and the New York Central agreed to a running time of 20 hours (the New York Central had previously made the run in 18 hours). In 1932, the two roads agreed to a time of 18 hours, and in 1935 it was reduced to 16.5 hours.

As we've noted, the New York Central always billed itself as the 'Water Level Route,' making the New York to Chicago run via the Hudson River Valley and Great Lakes country, while the Pennsylvania Railroad had to haul itself over the Appalachian Mountains. The *Water Level Express* was the New York Central's New York to Buffalo service.

Arrivals and departures of the *Twentieth Century Limited* came to be as exciting as those of transatlantic liners. A red carpet rolled out from the gate to the platform was the New York Central's way of telling passengers that they were special and could look forward to regal treatment in exchange for their extra fare. Many of the passengers were very special indeed. Celebrity hounds haunted the departure gate area hoping to see such notables of the day as movie stars Kate Smith and Gloria Swanson, politicians, sports figures and others. There was even a small group of aficionados who regularly rode the *Twentieth Century Limited* just to get a shave and a haircut—a form of dandyism that entered popular legend.

The post-World War II version of the *Twentieth Century Limited* was inaugu-

The *Magic Carpet* rolls out again

I**T'S CENTURY TIME!** A minute ago, outside the station, you were in the heart of a great city, with hurrying crowds, blaring taxis, newsboys shouting the evening headlines. Now you're in a different world as you follow that crimson carpet down the platform of Grand Central Terminal toward the softly lighted, streamlined cars that will be your club on wheels for tonight.

Relax by Twilight

Magically, the day's tension vanishes when you step into the Century's luxurious Observation car. Deep cushioned easy chairs invite you to relax. And outside the wide windows, the twilit beauty of the Water Level Route unrolls a background for repose.

The Face is Familiar

Beside superb cuisine and service, there's a fascination about dinner on this favorite train of famous people. For nearby may be a lovely face you last saw in technicolor, or a distinguished one that would be news on any financial page.

Awake Refreshed

You arrive looking and feeling your best. For all night, in the quiet privacy of your room, a spacious bed, a rubber-foam mattress, and the smooth Water Level Route have conspired to give you deep, refreshing sleep.

NEW YORK CENTRAL
The Water Level Route—You Can Sleep

The only all-room extra-fare train between New York and Chicago.

20TH CENTURY LIMITED

NEW YORK CENTRAL SYSTEM

Above: **The New York Central's classic *Water Level Express* glides along the famous 'Water Level Route' overlooking the Hudson River, circa 1919. The great *Twentieth Century Limited* would ply these same tracks en route to Chicago, but the *Water Level Express* was the New York to Buffalo run.**

rated in 1948 with a ceremony featuring the presence of Dwight D Eisenhower (not yet president) and singer Beatrice Lillie. The champagne bottle Miss Lillie smashed against the observation car was filled not with champagne but with waters from the Mohawk and Hudson rivers and from the Great Lakes. The observation car no longer had an open platform. Like the rest of the train, it was streamlined and featured an aerodynamically designed, curved rear end.

The ceremony around the newly modernized *Twentieth Century Limited* was supposed to herald a postwar era of prosperity for the New York Central. While the train was bright and new, those who rode ordinary New York Central trains could begin to see the unmistakable signs of deterioration.

In 1955, the *Twentieth Century Limited* sometimes had to run in several sections to handle the crowds, but on its first run, in 1902, it had only three Pullmans and 27

passengers. Even then, it had a barber-valet and a public stenographer, and it was one of the few trains to maintain those services into the 1950s. It also had private rooms with shower baths. The train secretary on the *Twentieth Century Limited* was both stenographer and telephone operator, and there was no charge for his services. Like the car phones of the 1990s, the telephone on the *Twentieth Century Limited* operated by radio to the nearest mobile exchange, then by wire and wireless to anywhere in the world, be it Tehran, Luxembourg, Mozambique or ships in mid-ocean.

Aside from the great *Twentieth Century Limited*, the *James Whitcomb Riley* was the last named train to remain in operation on the New York Central, when most such trains were terminated in 1967. The *James Whitcomb Riley* was a Cincinnati to Chicago daylight mile-a-minute streamliner, which also touched Indianapolis. Named for the great American

Above: **An early photograph of the fabled *Twentieth Century Limited*, dating from the days when the New York Central was still the New York Central & Hudson River.**

Below: **The Pennsylvania Railroad's classic *Senator* dashing down to Washington in May 1931. A few years later the lines would be electrified and this example of one of 'America's most beautiful daylight trains' would switch from steam to GG1 for its motive power.**

For a Carefree Vacation... GO BY TRAIN!

Yes, and like this little lady—go by Pennsylvania Railroad!

Our great passenger fleets offer a choice of 1,100 daily trains between East and West—North and South—scheduled for your convenience, equipped for your comfort... by day, by night. Whether you travel by sleeping car or coach, there is a train ready to take you when you are ready to go.

No better year—and no better way... whether you plan to visit New York, Washington or other eastern cities; a quiet resort, or the folks back home.

Enjoy the extra convenience and comforts the Pennsylvania Railroad now offers through its great network of through service. Coast-to-coast... to New England ... Eastern Canada... the South ... the Southwest —all without change of cars!

To the grandeur of the Canadian Rockies... to America's inspiring National Parks, well-timed connections.

Our city ticket offices, travel bureaus and ticket agents are available to help you plan a carefree and relaxed vacation—from the first to the final mile!

PENNSYLVANIA RAILROAD
Serving The Nation

Above: **As big as it was, the Pennsylvania Railroad never lost sight of the little things—at least not in its advertising! The classic streamliners of the Penney permitted connections with the classic streamliners of the nation.**

Opposite: **The classic *Jeffersonian* took you from the Hudson to the confluence of the Mississippi and Missouri, but best of all it promised you fun.**

poet who died in 1916, this train virtually defined luxury for the Chicago to Cincinnati route.

The New York Central also decided to put on a mile-a-minute freight between New York and Buffalo. Called the *Pacemaker*, it was mounted on passenger car trucks for smoother riding. However, before the cars were specially manufactured for it, a preliminary *Pacemaker* was assembled out of all the old baggage cars that could be scraped together. All blackened with soot, it was promptly christened *Blackbird* by the crews. However, when the new train was assembled with 75 to 80 cars all exactly alike—the upper half painted a delicate rose, the lower half gray—it was considered too beautiful to be nicknamed. The name *Pacemaker* was eventually assigned to a Chicago to New York passenger route.

A long-time Hudson River Valley commuter service, the *Bear Mountain* linked New York City with the state capital at Albany. Today, the route is one of many Amtrak lines connecting New York with Rensselaer, New York near Albany.

Named for the most famous resident of the two cities served, the *Benjamin Franklin* linked Philadelphia with Boston. One of many American trains with a 'spirit of '76' patriotic theme, the *Betsy Ross* linked New York and Washington, DC, via Ms Ross' hometown, Philadelphia. The New York Central launched its *Chicago Limited* in 1891, at the same time that George Daniels created the *Empire State Express* to run between New York and Buffalo. Daniels built the *Chicago Limited* into worldwide fame.

The New York Central had a *Commodore Vanderbilt* (as fast as the *Twentieth Century*), as well as a *Commodore II* and an *Advance Commodore Vanderbilt*. The streets of New York yielded several names, including *Broadway Limited* on the Pennsylvania, the New York Central's *Fifth Avenue Special*, the New Haven's *Forty-Second Street*, *Murray Hill* and *Pershing Square*, and the Reading-Jersey Central's *Wall Street*. For the city of Pittsburgh, there was the *Golden Triangle* on the Pennsylvania, and for Chicago the *La Salle Street Limited* on the Rock Island.

The New York Central's room-lounge-observation cars on streamliners were idyllically named for streams or islands—*Bedloe's Island*, *Bonnie Brook*, *Singing Brook*, *Rippling Stream*, *Crystal Stream*, *Manhattan Island*, and *Thousand Islands*. Meanwhile, the Pennsylvania Railroad's room-lounge-observation cars ran to 'Views'—*Skyline View*, *Metropolitan View*, *Federal View*, and *Washington View*. For room-bar-lounge facilities, it had 17 'Colonials.'

Today, Amtrak replicates the Pennsylvania's *Broadway Limited* with New York to Chicago service via Philadelphia, Pittsburgh and Cleveland. A supplementary train, called the *Pennsylvanian*, runs over the same track between New York and Philadelphia. At the same time, the old New York Central 'water level' route to Chicago is called the *Lake Shore Limited* in Amtrak's vernacular, and it also includes a Boston to Albany spur. Just as Amtrak's *Broadway Limited* is supplemented as far as Philadelphia by the *Pennsylvanian*, the *Lake Shore Limited* now shares the rails with Amtrak's 'Empire Service' between New York and Buffalo.

NOW...
A Complete <u>RECREATION CAR</u>

**Especially Designed
for Your Pleasure**

*A diagrammatic painting
of Pennsylvania Railroad's
new recreation car.*

In daily service on The Jeffersonian, popular all-coach streamliner between New York and St. Louis!
A dramatic highlight in Pennsylvania Railroad's new equipment program, this colorful new recreation car provides amusement and entertainment for all ages. A luxurious game and reading lounge . . . a children's playroom . . . a sunken buffet lounge . . . miniature movie theatre—pleasure *with variety*. Be among the first to enjoy it! Reserve a seat on *The Jeffersonian* on your next trip!

Enjoy these New Features at Low Coach Fares!
THE JEFFERSONIAN

Westbound

Lv. New York	6:15 P.M.
Lv. Philadelphia	7:43 P.M.
Lv. Washington	6:20 P.M.
Lv. Baltimore	7:05 P.M.
Lv. Harrisburg	9:42 P.M.
Ar. Columbus	6:46 A.M.
Ar. Dayton	8:21 A.M.
Ar. Indianapolis	9:27 A.M.
Ar. St. Louis	1:50 P.M.

Eastbound

Lv. St. Louis	1:00 P.M.
Lv. Indianapolis	5:07 P.M.
Lv. Dayton	8:13 P.M.
Lv. Columbus	9:35 P.M.
Ar. Harrisburg	6:51 A.M.
Ar. Baltimore	9:23 A.M.
Ar. Washington	10:10 A.M.
Ar. Philadelphia	8:52 A.M.
Ar. New York	10:25 A.M.

Recreation car facilities available to Baltimore and Washington passengers between Harrisburg and St. Louis.

SO ROOMY AND RESTFUL—the new overnight coaches on *The Jeffersonian*. Only 44 seats to the car—and all reclining! You'll like the new lighting, too—fluorescent, 4 times brighter but easy on the eyes. New-type air-conditioning adds still more comfort.

EXTRA LARGE MODERN WASHROOMS, one for women, one for men at the end of each coach—handsomely decorated—with 3 glistening washstands and 2 toilet annexes.

PENNSYLVANIA RAILROAD
Serving the Nation

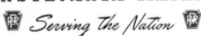

ROADS SOUTH OF CHICAGO

Below: No matter where you went, it always seemed that the trains that inspired the most memorable songs were the ones that ran south out of Chicago. There was the *Wabash Cannonball*, of course, and the Illinois Central's great *City of New Orleans*—the 'Magic Carpet Made of Steel'—seen here.

Opposite: Seen here in the stark midsummer light at Jackson, Mississippi, is another great Illinois Central classic, the *Panama Limited*.

The Illinois Central was called the 'Main Line of Mid-America,' and the *City of New Orleans* was its flagship. The *City of New Orleans* was the grandest of America's classic streamliners. For many it was *the* classic American streamliner. It ran from Chicago south across the rich farmlands of Illinois to the Mississippi River at Cairo, Illinois, and down through Memphis, Tennessee, and Jackson, Mississippi. From there the line ran—in the words of Steve Goodman in his stirring song about this greatest of streamliners—'Through the Mississippi Delta, rollin' down to the sea.'

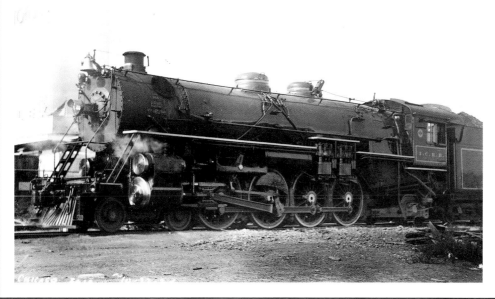

The Illinois Central was founded in 1857 with the first railroad land grant in America, which was issued by Millard Fillmore, and it was charted to cover the ground its name describes. The first line that was built connected the Mississippi River port of Cairo, Illinois, with Chicago via Springfield in the Illinois heartland. Eventually, lines were built west across Iowa and south to New Orleans.

More recently, the Illinois Central, which was merged with the Gulf, Mobile & Ohio in 1940, became a mere subsidiary of a conglomerate called Illinois Central Industries, which proceeded to strip it of half of its tracks. However, in 1989, through a corporate restructuring, ties were severed and a brand new Illinois Central Railroad began afresh on the same fertile ground where it had originally taken root 150 years before.

Above: **This little vest pocket folder from the 1950s is a veritable encyclopedia of Illinois Central classics. The great *City of New Orleans* runs in Amtrak colors today, and the sons of Pullman porters and the sons of engineers can recall their fathers' magic carpet made of steel.**

Below: **The Illinois Central's *Green Diamond* made the run to St Louis by day, while the *Night Diamond* left at 9:45 pm and offered sleepers.**

Meanwhile, the *City of New Orleans* is still operated between Chicago and the Crescent City by Amtrak, completing 924 miles in 18 hours.

A sister train to the Illinois Central's famous *City of New Orleans*, the *Panama Limited* did not serve Panama or even Panama City, Florida, but rather the same Chicago to New Orleans route as the *City of New Orleans*. The name dates to the era of the construction of the Panama Canal, a milestone in early twentieth century American history, and a time when people working on the canal traveled from Chicago to New Orleans to board ships bound for Panama. Illinois Central's *Louisiane* also ran to New Orleans via Memphis, and the *City of Miami* connected Chicago with that destination.

The Illinois Central, in addition to local place names, honored its territory with *King Coal, King Cotton, Sugarland, Hawkeye, Timberland, Pelican State, Land o' Corn* and the amusing *Land o' Strawberries*. There were trains named for Native American tribes, such as the Chicago to St Petersburg *Seminole*, and the St Louis or Louisville to Memphis *Chickasaw*. Beginning around 1910, there was a local train on the Illinois Central in Mississippi called the *Ripper*. A famous story is told of a conductor named Gaerig who was running between Gwin, Mississippi and Memphis, Tennessee. At the time of the story, the through freight made the run several hours quicker than the local, but the crews' pay was the same for both, so crews alternated. Gaerig had somehow drawn the local job several times in succession, so he went

into the dispatcher's office at Gwin one day and said, sarcastically, 'I'm ready for that *Rip Track Special*.' This was an allusion to the fact that cars headed for the 'rip,' or repair track, had to be moved slowly because of their mechanical defects. The quip was abbreviated to *The Ripper*, and so the train was known for nearly half a century.

In 1880, the grand old Alton Railroad had initiated its *Alton Limited* Chicago to St Louis run, which it modestly admitted was the 'handsomest train in the world,' though others which survived until the 1950s challenged its magnificence. In 1889, the Chicago & Alton Railroad started a train known as the *Hummer* and ran it between Chicago and Kansas City for half a century.

In the South were the Florida East Coast's *Gulf Stream* and the *Gulf Wind*, operated jointly with the Louisville & Nashville and the Seaboard Air Line. The Columbus & Greenville Railroad once had a *Deltan* (the Yazoo Delta, not the Mississippi) passenger train, but eventually that road dropped its passenger service and turned to running freight trains exclusively.

There was also a little logging road called the Yazoo Delta Railroad. It had yellow cars, and even some of the locomotives were yellow. Making up a train one day, an Illinois Central yardmaster had to take over some cars from that road and said, 'All right, now let's get this *Yellow Dog* moving,' thus unintentionally naming his own train. It is possibly coincidental that the road's initials were YD.

The Central of Georgia, which cooperated with its 'big sister,' the Illinois Central, to operate the *Seminole* and *City of Miami* operated the renowned *Dixie Flyer*, as well as the *Georgian*.

Named for America's sixteenth president, the *Abraham Lincoln* was one of the Gulf, Mobile & Ohio's great streamliners. It operated between Chicago and St Louis until Amtrak took over all of Gulf, Mobile & Ohio's passenger service in the early 1970s.

The Gulf, Mobile & Ohio also had a train known as *The Rebel*, whose name proved highly controversial. The management feebly tried to deny to skeptical Northern travel agents that it referred to the gray-coated soldiers of the War Between the States, but, as might be expected, nobody was convinced.

There was a pleasantly old South, small-town touch in the Gulf, Mobile &

45

Ohio's *Judge Milton Brown*. Despite this homey touch, foreigners were not forgotten. There was also the *Marco Polo*, *Christopher Columbus*, *George Stephenson*, *Henry Bessemer*, *Alfred Nobel* and *Roentgen*.

The Louisville & Nashville was a marvelous 'old South' road with its wonderfully genteel *Azalean* from Pittsburgh to Pensacola and New Orleans by way of Memphis or Birmingham. Also on the Louisville & Nashville was the *Humming Bird* that ran between Cincinnati and New Orleans. Hank Williams—that is Hank *Sr*—even wrote a song about the Louisville & Nashville's *Pan-American* that wandered down to New Orleans from New York by way of Cincinnati with Pennsylvania Railroad connections. However, the greatest of the Louisville & Nashville's streamliners ran on its flagship routes from Chicago to Miami. These enlisted the aid of both the Pennsylvania Railroad and the Baltimore & Ohio, and included the *Southland* via Detroit and Cincinnati, the *Flamingo* via Detroit and Atlanta and that true classic, the *South Wind*, which traveled through Louisville and Montgomery. In 1937, the Louisville & Nashville took a literary turn in the naming of its rolling stock and sponsored cars named *James Lane Allen*, *John James Audubon*, *Stephen Collins Foster*, *Sidney Lanier*, *Theodore O'Hara* (author of *The Bivouac of the Dead*), and *Sam Davis* (the so-called 'Confederate Nathan Hale').

The Wabash Railway, organized in 1915 from components dating back to 1837,

ran from Kansas City to Buffalo, New York, with spurs and loops serving cities such as Chicago, Omaha and St Louis. The *Wabash Cannonball*, the most famous of the Wabash passenger trains, was the daytime route between Detroit and St Louis.

The classic Chicago to Urbana, Illinois, a sister train to the Wabash Railway's *Wabash Cannonball*, the *Banner Blue* ran from Chicago to St Louis as a sort of understudy to the Wabash's *Blue Bird*. The *Blue Bird* was actually the Wabash Railway's most popular streamliner, running from Chicago to St Louis using the best Wabash equipment. In the 1950s, this included Vista-Dome cars. It is worth a mention that the *Banner Blue* was probably the last train in America to feature an open platform parlor observation car.

Above: **The classic *City of Miami* left Miami in the late afternoon, and had you in Chicago for breakfast on the second day.**

Below: **The Southern Railway's *Southerner* left New Orleans in the early morning, reached Atlanta by evening, and connected with the Pennsylvania Railroad in Washington, as seen here, by breakfast time.**

Illinois Central Railroad

Main Line of Mid-America

PULLMAN, COACH AND DINING CAR SERVICE

REGULARLY ASSIGNED CARS ARE AIR-CONDITIONED

All passenger trains shown herein carry coaches, except as indicated otherwise.

SOUTHBOUND

THE CITY OF NEW ORLEANS. Daily
Diesel-Powered Coach Streamliner.
Deluxe Reclining Seats—Stewardess—
Radio—Tavern Lounge—Observation Car.

No. 1—Chicago to New Orleans—Table 1
No. 201-1—St. Louis to New Orleans—Table 12

Dining Car Service—Chicago to New Orleans.

Coaches—Chicago to New Orleans.
St. Louis to New Orleans (No. 1 from Carbondale).
St. Louis to Carbondale.

No. 3—THE LOUISIANE. No. 103—IRVIN S. COBB. Daily
No. 3—Chicago to New Orleans—Table 1
No. 103-15-3—Louisville to New Orleans—Table 13

Sleepers—
Chicago to Memphis, Tenn., 8-Sec., 5 Double Bedrooms [301].
Chicago to Memphis, 18 Roomette [303].
Cincinnati to Memphis, 10-Section, 1 Compartment, 1 D.R. [1031].
(B. & O No. 6; Cincinnati to Louisville, No. 103 Louisville to Fulton and No. 15 to Memphis.) (Occupancy at Memphis until 8 00 a.m.)
Louisville to Paducah, Ky., 8-Section, Drawing-room, 2 Compartment, [1033]. (May be occupied at Paducah until 7 00 a.m.)

Diner—Chicago to Champaign. Fulton to Memphis.

Illinois Central Parlor - Lounge Car—(Radio).
Chicago to Memphis [307]. (Pullman Tickets.)

Coaches—Chicago to New Orleans.
Louisville to Memphis (No. 15 from Fulton).

THE PANAMA LIMITED. Daily
Diesel-Powered Streamlined Train.
All Pullman Train—Radio—Valet—No Coaches.
No. 5—Chicago to New Orleans—Table 1
No. 205-5—St. Louis to New Orleans—Table 12

Sleepers—
Chicago to New Orleans, 6-Sec., 6 Roomette, 4 Double Bedroom [519].
Chicago to New Orleans, 6-Sec., 6 Roomette, 4 Double Bedroom [517].
Chicago to New Orleans, 10 Roomette, 5 Double Bedroom [515].
Chicago to New Orleans, 10 Roomette, 6 Double Bedroom [523].

Club Lounge—Chicago to New Orleans.

Diner—Twin Unit. Chicago to New Orleans.

Sleepers—
Chicago to New Orleans, 2 Drawing-room, 4 Compartment, 4 Double Bedroom [511].
Chicago to New Orleans, 10 Roomette, 6 Double Bedroom [509].

Parlor Car—
Chicago to Carbondale [PC]—(Illinois Central Tickets).

Sleepers—
St. Louis to New Orleans, 10 Roomette, 6 Double Bedroom [507]. (No. 5 Carbondale to New Orleans.)
St. Louis to New Orleans, 6-Section, 6 Roomette, 4 Double Bedroom [505]. (No. 5 Carbondale to New Orleans.)
Memphis to New Orleans, 6-Section, 6 Roomette, 4 Double Bedroom [551]. (Open for occupancy 9 30 p.m.)
Chicago to Jackson, Miss., 6-Section, 6 Roomette, 4 Double Bedroom [503]. (May be occupied at Jackson, Miss., until 8 00 a.m.)

Parlor Car—
Jackson to New Orleans [PC-5]—(Illinois Central Tickets).

Sleeper—
Chicago to New Orleans, 2 Double Bedroom, 1 Drawing-room, 2 Compartment-Observation [501].

Buffet-Lounge Car—(RADIO.) Sandwiches—Refreshments (St. Louis to Carbondale)—[2051]—(Illinois Central Parlor Car). I. C. tickets. (Diner No. 5 Carbondale to New Orleans.)

Coaches—St. Louis to Carbondale (on No. 205).

Nearly half a century after air travel began to take its toll on railroads, new trains were being added in the United States. In the 1980s, the owners of Europe's *Nostalgie Istanbul Orient Express*—which sought to recreate the magic of the original *Orient Express*—joined forces with Florida real estate interests to create an American luxury train with vintage Pullman cars and a European flavor. The train, the *American-European Express*, now makes evening runs between Washington, DC, and Chicago. Each train consists of five cars—three sleeping cars, a dining car and a club car—designed for a mere 56 passengers. The cars bear either American or European place names—hence, among the present company fleet, there are sleepers named *Washington*, *Paris*, *Vienna*, *Istanbul*, *Monte Carlo* and *Berlin*. The two diners currently on the company roster are named *Zurich* and *Chicago*; and the two club cars are *Bay Point* and *St Moritz*.

The company undertook extensive renovation of unused Pullman cars—down to the installation of undercarriage equipment utilizing new technology—to assure a smooth, quiet ride. Upgraded heating, air conditioning, plumbing and other refinements were also made to the cars. Luxuriant interiors with an Art Deco flair were commissioned. Dark mahogany, tastefully bordered and highlighted with brass and inlay work, was chosen as the base for these interiors. Brass lighting fixtures, marble surfaces and painted ceiling murals added further notes of adornment. Period fabrics, echoing the tastes of the 1920s and 1930s—worsted wools, damask cottons and linens in shades of mauve, teal and brown—were selected for curtains, upholstery and wall coverings. Soft, embossed leathers were picked to cover the walls of the club cars. Rich and subtle carpeting was chosen for the floors. The Drexel Heritage firm designed tables, chairs and other period furniture for the diners and club cars. Original paintings were commissioned. There is even an onboard FAX and telephone service.

Each sleeping car has a shower, and all sleeping compartments are equipped with a private 'water closet' and a sink. Mahogany, leather and fine fabrics, plus room lighting and reading lamps, highlight the sleeping quarters.

Ebony armchairs provide seating in the dining cars, which feature an executive dining room in addition to the beautiful regular dining section. Linen tablecloths, fine crystal, brass trim, mahogany paneling and European (oversized) silverware combine to create an atmosphere of warmth and impeccable taste. A full selection of European and American wines, port and cognac, and a seven course gourmet dinner menu (plus a la carte selections)—prepared by the *chef de cuisine* and his staff, in the full kitchen that occupies the rear of the dining car—add up to a high level of dining satisfaction.

The average fare for a journey on the *American-European Express* is less than air travel plus a night at a hotel and the cost of comparable meals. This service is a splendid alternative to ordinary travel accommodations in the Washington-Chicago corridor and a marvelous way to recapture the enchantment of a bygone age.

Today on the rails south of Chicago, Amtrak has, of course, retained the *City*

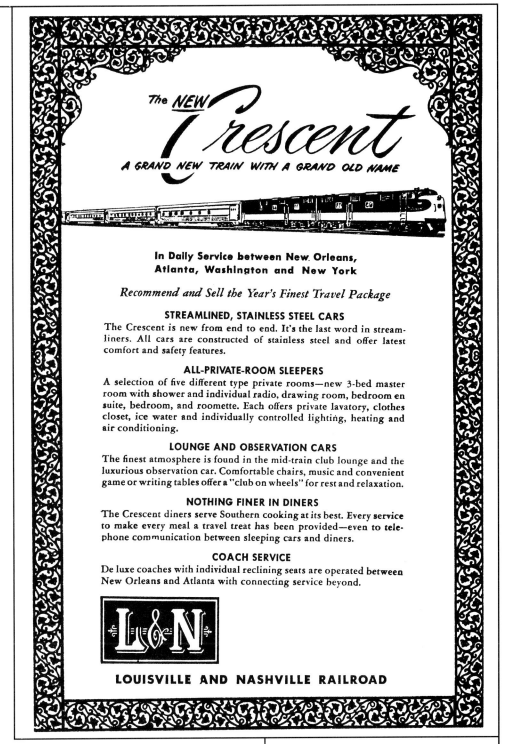

of New Orleans as one of its flagship routes. The flock of *Eagles* (*Texas Eagle*, *Colorado Eagle*, *Louisiana Eagle*, etc) that used to fly for Missouri Pacific's Texas & Pacific subsidiary are now amalgamated as Amtrak's *Texas Eagle*. Today's *Texas Eagle* runs from Chicago to Dallas via St Louis and then forks, with one spur to San Antonio via Fort Worth and Austin and another to Houston. Amtrak operates another train on the ground once tread by *Eagles* and *Rockets* which is now known as *River Cities*. It parallels the Missouri River from Kansas City to St Louis, and the Mississippi from St Louis to New Orleans.

Above: **The Louisville & Nashville's classic *Crescent* took it's name from New Orleans—the Crescent City—and from the route that it took, which ironically bypassed both Louisville and Nashville.**

Opposite: **Just as the Louisville & Nashville's *Crescent* bypassed both Louisville and Nashville, the Illinois Central's *Panama Limited* served neither Panama nor Panama City, Florida. Actually, both trains served New Orleans. The name *Panama Limited* originated when the train took people down from Chicago to catch Panama-bound steamers during the building of the Canal.**

THE EASTERN SEABOARD TRAINS

The longest-lived train in America—excluding Amtrak's current use of classic names—was possibly the Fall River Line's *Steamboat Express*, which ran on the Old Colony Railroad and its successor, the New York, New Haven & Hartford. The *Steamboat Express* began operating alongside the famous Fall River Line of overnight boats between New York and Fall River. The 'Boat Train,' as it was popularly known, left Boston at 5:00 pm and dashed down to Fall River in an hour, stopping alongside the boat. In 1853, its time of departure was changed to 5:30 and in 1875 to 6:00 pm.

This remained constant until the 1940s, except for some variations during the Spanish-American War and World War I. When the Fall River Line boats ceased operation in 1937, the *Boat Train* also halted forever, after 90 years of uninterrupted service.

The Old Colony launched another famous train in 1884, a three- or four-coach, extra fare, private car system, that left Boston on summer afternoons at 3:00 pm and skittered over the 72 miles to Woods Hole in an hour and a half so that bankers and businessmen, closing their roll-top desks a little early, could eat supper at the Sea View Hotel in Martha's Vineyard as early as 6:00 pm. It was promptly nicknamed by railroaders the *Dude Train*, and so it continued to be known, quite matter-of-factly, until the National Railroad Administration—which took over the railroads during World War I—abolished it in 1918.

Between Boston and Washington, meanwhile, the *Washington Night Express* was launched by the New York, New Haven & Hartford Railroad in 1876, principally because of the Centennial Exposition at Philadelphia. Bypassing Manhattan, it carried a big car ferry nine

BALTIMORE & OHIO RAILROAD

PULLMAN, COACH AND DINING CAR SERVICE
Coaches on All Trains, except No. 5 Washington to Chicago and No. 6 Chicago to Washington.

WESTWARD

No. 1—THE NATIONAL LIMITED—Daily.
Sun Room-Observation Lounge Car..Washington to St. Louis—3-Compartments, 1-Drawing-room. (Buffet.) (Radio.)
Sleeping Cars..New York to St. Louis—10-Section, 2-Compts., 1-D.R.
New York to Louisville—8-Section, 5 Double Bedrooms. (No. 57 from Cincinnati.)
Washington to St. Louis—14-Section.
Washington to St. Louis and San Antonio—14-Roomettes, 4 Double Bedrooms. (Frisco-Katy No. 1 from St. Louis.)
Washington to St. Louis and Fort Worth—14 Roomettes, 4 Dble. Bdrms. (Mo. Pac.- T. & P. No. 1 from St. Louis.)
Dining Car.....New York to St. Louis.
Coach Lounge Car..Washington to St. Louis.
Reclining Seat Coaches..New York to St. Louis.
New York to St. Louis.
Washington to St. Louis (Lounge Rooms). (Seats reserved in advance without charge from Washington and Silver Spring to Cincinnati and west.)
Diesel-Electric all the way.
Stewardess—Washington to St. Louis.

No. 3—THE DIPLOMAT—Daily.
Lounge Car....New York to St Louis—8-Section. (Buffet.) (Radio.)
Sleeping Cars..New York to St. Louis—14-Roomettes, 4 Double Bdrms.
New York to St. Louis—8-Section, 4 Double Bedrooms.
New York to Louisville—12-Section, 1-Drawing-room. (No. 51 from North Vernon.)
Dining Car....New York to St. Louis.
Coach Lounge Car..New York to St. Louis.
Reclining Seat Coach..New York to St. Louis (with Women's Lounge).
Diesel-Electric all the way.
Stewardess—Washington to St. Louis.

No. 5—THE CAPITOL LIMITED—Daily.
Club Car ......Washington to Chicago. (Buffet.) (Radio.)
Observation Lounge Car..Washington to Chicago—5 Double Bedrooms. (Buffet.) (Radio.)
Strata Dome Car..Washington to Chicago—5 Roomettes, 1 Single Bedroom, 3 Drawing-rooms.
Lounge Car....Washington to Chicago—8-Section. (Buffet.) (Radio.)
Sleeping Cars..New York to Chicago—14-Roomettes, 4 Double Bedrooms.
New York to Chicago—8-Section, 5 Double Bedrooms.
Washington to Chicago—10- Roomettes, 6-Double Bedrooms. (4 cars.)
Washington to Chicago—14-Section.
Washington to Chicago—12-Section, 1-Drawing-room.
Washington to Los Angeles and San Diego—10 Roomettes, 6 Double Bedrooms. (Santa Fe No. 19—74 from Chicago.)
Dining Cars....New York to Washington. Washington to Chicago.
Parlor Car (Sleeper)..New York to Washington—Drawing-room.
Coach Lounge Car..New York to Washington.
Reclining Seat Coach (Lounge Rooms)..New York to Chicago. (No. 25 from Washington). (Seats reserved in advance to Pittsburgh and west.)
Diesel-Electric all the way.
All-Pullman (with Train Secretary), Washington to Chicago.

No. 7—THE SHENANDOAH—Daily.
Lounge Car....New York to Chicago—8 Section. (Buffet.) (Radio.)
Strata Dome Car..Washington to Chicago (on odd dates)—5 Roomettes, 1 Single Bedroom, 3 Drawing-rooms.
Sleeping Cars..New York to Chicago—10-Sec. 2-Compts., 1-D.R.
New York to Pittsburgh—8-Sec., 1-D.R., 3 Dble. Bdrms. (May be occupied in Pittsburgh until 8 00 a.m.)
Washington to Chicago—10-Section, 2-Compts., 1-D.R. (Open 10 00 p.m.)
Washington to Pittsburgh—17 Roomettes (Sunday, Tuesday, Thursday) or 12 Roomettes, 1 Single Bedroom, 4 Double Bedrooms (Monday, Wednesday, Friday). (Open 10 00 p.m.) (May be occupied in Pittsburgh until 8 00 a.m.)
Washington to Pittsburgh—10-Sec., 3 Double Bedrooms. (Open 10 00 p.m.) (May be occupied in Pittsburgh until 8 00 a.m.)
Dining Cars....New York to Washington. Pittsburgh to Chicago.
Parlor Car (Sleeper)..New York to Washington (Drawing-room).
Coach Lounge Car..New York to Chicago.
Reclining Seat Coach..New York to Chicago. (With Women's Lounge.)
Diesel-Electric all the way.
Stewardess—Washington to Chicago.

EASTWARD

No. 2—THE NATIONAL LIMITED—Daily.
Sun Room-Observation Lounge Car..St. Louis to Washington—3-Compartments, 1-Drawing-room. (Buffet.) (Radio.)
Lounge Car...Washington to New York. (Buffet.) (Radio.)
Sleeping Cars..St. Louis to New York—14-Roomettes, 4 Dbl. Bedrooms.
St. Louis to New York—10-Sec., 2-Compts., 1-D.R.
St. Louis to Washington—14-Section.
Louisville to New York—8-Section, 5 Double Bedrooms. (No. 50 to North Vernon).
San Antonio and St. Louis to Washington—14-Roomettes, 4 Double Bedrooms. (Katy-Frisco No. 2 to St. Louis.)
Fort Worth and St. Louis to Washington—14 Roomettes, 4 Dble. Bdrms. (T. & P.-Mo. Pac. No. 2 to St. Louis.)
Pittsburgh to New York—8-Section, 1-Drawing-room, 3 Double Bedrooms. (No. 10 to Washington.)
Dining Car.....St. Louis to New York.
Coach Lounge Car..St. Louis to New York.
Reclining Seat Coach..St. Louis to New York (Lounge Rooms). (Seats reserved in advance without charge from Cincinnati and west to Silver Spring and Washington.)
Diesel-Electric all the way.
Stewardess—St. Louis to Washington.

No. 4—THE DIPLOMAT—Daily.
Lounge Car....St. Louis to New York—8-Section. (Buffet.) (Radio.)
Sleeping Cars..St. Louis to New York—14-Roomettes, 4 Double Bedrooms.
Louisville to N. Y.—12-Sec., 1-D.R. (52 to North Vernon.)
Dining Car.....St. Louis to New York.
Coach Lounge Car..St. Louis to New York.
Reclining Seat Coach..St. Louis to New York (with Women's Lounge).
Diesel-Electric all the way.
Stewardess—St. Louis to Washington.

No. 6—THE CAPITOL LIMITED—Daily.
Club Car.......Chicago to Washington. (Buffet.) (Radio.)
Observation Lounge Car..Chicago to Washington—5 Double Bedrooms. (Buffet.) (Radio.)
Strata Dome Car..Chicago to Washington—5 Roomettes, 1 Single Bedroom, 3 Drawing-rooms.
Lounge Car....Chicago to Washington—8-Section. (Buffet.) (Radio.)
Sleeping Cars..San Diego and Los Angeles to Washington—10 Roomettes, 6 Double Bedrooms. (Santa Fe 71—20 to Chicago.)
Chicago to New York—14-Roomettes, 4 Dble. Bedrooms.
Chicago to New York—8-Section, 4 Double Bedrooms.
Chicago to Washington—10 Roomettes, 6 Double Bedrooms. (4 cars.)
Chicago to Washington—12-Section, 1-Drawing-room.
Chicago to Washington—14-Section.
Dining Cars....Chicago to Washington. Washington to New York.
Parlor Car (Sleeper)..Washington to New York—Drawing-room.
Coach Lounge Car..Washington to New York.
Reclining Seat Coach (Lounge Rooms)..Chicago to New York. (No. 26 to Washington.)
Diesel-Electric all the way.
All-Pullman (with Train Secretary), Chicago to Washington.

No. 8—THE SHENANDOAH—Daily.
Lounge Car....Chicago to New York—8-Section. (Buffet.) (Radio.)
Strata Dome Car..Chicago to Washington (on even dates)—5 Roomettes, 1 Single Bedroom, 3 Drawing-rooms. (Open 9 30 p.m.)
Sleeping Cars..Chicago to Akron—8-Sec., 4 Dble. B. R. (Open to 8 00 a.m.)
Chicago to Pittsburgh—8-Section, 2-Compt., 1-D.R.
(Open 9 30 p.m.) Chicago to Pittsburgh—10-Roomettes, 5 Double Bedrooms (except Saturday).
Chicago to Washington—10-Section, 2-Compts., 1-D.R.
Chicago to New York—10-Section, 2-Compts., 1-D.R.
Dining Cars....Youngstown to Washington. Washington to New York.
Coach Lounge Car..Chicago to New York.
Reclining Seat Coach (Open 10 00 p.m.)..Chicago to New York (with Women's Lounge).
Diesel-Electric all the way.
Stewardess—Chicago to Washington.

No. 10—CHICAGO-PITTSBURGH-WASHINGTON EXPRESS—Daily.
Lounge Car....Chicago to Washington—8-Section. (Buffet.) (Radio.) (May be occupied until 7 30 a.m.)
Sleeping Cars..Chicago to Washington—10-Section, 2-Compt., 1-D.R. (May be occupied until 7 30 a.m.)
Pittsburgh to New York—8-Sec, 1 D.R., 3 Double Bedrooms. (Open 9 00 p.m.) (No. 2 from Washington.)
Dining Car.....Chicago to Pittsburg.
Reclining Seat Coach..Chicago to Washington.
Diesel-Electric all the way.

Regularly assigned cars on all through trains are Air-Conditioned.

---

tion. Other notable classics on the New York, New Haven & Hartford included the *Narragansett*, the *Nathan Hale*, the *Yankee Clipper* and several others named for New York City destinations such as the *Murray Hill* and the *Forty-Second Street*.

In New England there was Boston & Maine's great *Flying Yankee, Skipper* and *Beachcomber*, the New York, New Haven and Hartford's *Yankee Clipper, Nutmeg* and *Puritan* and its two Cape Cod trains, *Cranberry* and *Sand Dune*. In addition to its *Flying Yankee*, the Boston & Maine ran the memorable *Connecticut Yankee, State of Maine*, and, of course, the *Minute Man*. (The Boston & Maine's slogan was 'The Route of the *Minute Man*'.) Working harmoniously with Canada's rival Canadian National and Canadian Pacific, the Boston & Maine ran a portfolio of trains between Boston and Montreal, including the *New Englander* and *Red Wing* that involved both Canadian roads, as well as the *Gull* (with Canadian National) and the *Alouette* (with Canadian Pacific). Boston & Maine also had a link in the Washington to Montreal streamliners *Washingtonian* and *Montrealer*.

As the nation's capital, Washington, DC, was always a railroad passenger hub, but as late as the 1920s, it still had the ambience of a sleepy Southern town. It was more like Richmond or Nashville than New York City or Philadelphia. This rapidly changed after 1933 when Franklin D Roosevelt became president. His New Deal program greatly increased the size of government and hence the number of bureaucrats and lobbyists traveling in and out of Washington's grand Union Station. With the entry of the United States into World War II in 1941, the federal government grew larger still. Not only did the size of the military increase, but new civilian organizations were formed to serve the war effort. Then too gasoline rationing took people out of their cars and put them on the trains.

The railroad companies noted Washington's importance as a terminus and named their trains to capture this mood. The Baltimore & Ohio had its *Ambassador, Capitol Limited, Diplomat* and *National Limited*.

In 1952, the Baltimore & Ohio introduced its 'Strata-Dome' cars on the *Capitol Limited*, as well as on the *Columbian* and *Shenandoah*.

The Chesapeake & Ohio, along with the Baltimore & Ohio (with which it later merged) used the national capital as a

miles across the river between the New Haven tracks in the Bronx and Jersey City. This train—whose name was changed in 1892 to the *Federal Express*—ran for 30 years before it became all-rail, going from New Haven via Danbury, the Poughkeepsie Bridge and Trenton to Philadelphia, and continued to do good business despite this long detour. When the Hell Gate Bridge across the East River was opened in 1913, the *Federal Express* began taking a direct course through Pennsylvania Station in New York City. Ultimately known merely as the *Federal*, it won notoriety in 1952 by crashing into Washington's Union Sta-

hub. Claiming descent from the 1785 canal project by which George Washington had hoped to connect Virginia with the Ohio Valley, the Chesapeake & Ohio chose names for its cars that rolled delightfully from the annuals of early American history, laying stress on anything connected with Washington—*American Revolution, Spirit of '76, Valley Forge, First Citizen, Commander-in-Chief, Pohick Church,* which was attended by the first president, *Tobias Lear* (his secretary), *Lord Fairfax* (his early employer), and some of his comrades-in-arms, such as *Marquis Lafayette, Count de Rochambeau, Baron von Steuben,* and even his gallant enemy, *Lord Cornwallis. Brother Jonathan* was there, too, and *Pierre L'Enfant,* who designed the city of Washington, and *Jack Jouett,* who rode to warn Thomas Jefferson that Tarleton and his cavalry were coming with intent to capture him. Then, too, the road had a streamliner called *George Washington,* of all names, on the Washington to Cincinnati run!

The Chesapeake & Ohio's restaurant cars were named for famous old taverns in the Washington country such as *Michie's Tavern,* built by Patrick Henry's father, *Gadsby's Tavern* in Washington and *Union Tavern* in Georgetown, whose guest lists included all the early presidents, statesmen and diplomats.

The Chesapeake & Ohio also honored *Pere Marquette,* while the New York Central and the Boston & Maine each had a *Paul Revere,* and the New Haven remembered *Nathan Hale.* The Pennsylvania naturally had a *William Penn.*

The spring of 1889 saw the birth of another famous train when the Chesapeake & Ohio seized upon the initials of the 'First Families of Virginia' and named a new golden yellow speedster the *Fast Flying Virginian,* or in common usage, the *FFV.*

The Chesapeake & Ohio also paid a great deal of attention to pioneer Kentucky, naming cars after *Isaac Shelby, Simon Kenton, James Harrod, Kentucky Home* (the state song), and, of course, *Anne Bailey,* who, when her husband was killed in the Point Pleasant battle with the Native Americans in 1774, donned male attire and became a valued scout and messenger. Most humble of all was *Ann McGinty,* who brought the first spinning wheel into the Kentucky wilderness. On a loom built by her husband, she spun and wove the first linen in Kentucky, from the lint of nettles and the first linsey-woolsey cloth, from nettle-lint and buffalo wool.

The New Haven, on the other hand, came right out frankly and named a car *Wall Street.* Supposing, on a broiling hot day, you looked forward to a cool seat in a parlor car, would you be daunted at discovering that the car is the *Sally Ann Furnace?*

The Chesapeake & Ohio's chief rival and eventual merger partner was, of course, the Baltimore & Ohio, whose grandest streamliners were sisters known as the *National Limited* and the *Capitol Limited.* The latter operated between Washington and Chicago, and was to the Baltimore & Ohio what the *Broad-*

Below: **The Philadelphia & Reading offered service featuring the *Crusader*, a powerful, yet streamlined, 4-6-2. The Philadelphia & Reading's classic trains were the *Black Diamond* that ran from Philadelphia to Buffalo by way of Mauch Chunk and Wilkes-Barre, and the *Interstate Express*, which linked Philadelphia with Syracuse. Reading itself was served by a local that ran to Pottsville.**

The Philadelphia & Reading was dependant upon connections with the Baltimore & Ohio for access to the rest of the East, but it offered the larger road access to its vital seashore lines.

way Limited was to the Pennsylvania Railroad, and the *Twentieth Century Limited* was to the New York Central.

Great American history was made along the route traveled by the Baltimore & Ohio's *Capitol Limited*. The train passed by Philadelphia, where Betsy Ross designed the Stars and Stripes and where the Liberty Bell is enshrined in Independence Hall. She served Washington, DC, with its stately buildings and monuments visible from the cars, and Harper's Ferry, where three states and two rivers meet in the Blue Ridge Mountains of West Virginia, and where John Brown's savage raid in 1859 cut the pattern for the War Between the States.

After dark, the *Capitol Limited*'s observation car, the Strata-Dome, used a powerful floodlight to illuminate the scenery, presenting vignettes of countryside in the path of light, until the light was paled by the glare of Pittsburgh's sprawling steel mills. Today, the *Capitol Limited* lives on as an Amtrak streamliner running the same route from Washington, Pittsburgh and Cleveland to Chicago.

The Baltimore & Ohio was also famous in the first half of the twentieth century for providing all-expenses-paid rail tours to Washington, DC, for high school and other civic groups, and a private car bearing such a privileged entourage was often picked up at the United States capital by the *Capitol Limited*.

Sometimes it is impossible to learn just how a nickname began. The Baltimore & Ohio had two freights nicknamed *Dirty Shirt*, and one would expect to find the origin of such a colorful tag on the tip of somebody's tongue, but both go back into the misty depths of the early twentieth century, and the reason for these trains having their names is unknown. One train running in the Ohio and Indiana area that was so named is believed to have been christened by two assistant trainmasters who had to ride it frequently, to the detriment of their linen. The train which ambled down the main line below Cumberland had the job of picking up and taking care of cars set out by other trains because of hot boxes or other defects. Since it did a lot of dirty work, it was called *Dirty Shirt*.

The origins of other names are more obvious. So named for the mountains through which it ran, the once-great *Adirondack* served the Montreal to New York route. Today, the *Adirondack* wears Amtrak colors and provides service through the Hudson River Valley between New York and Montreal's Gare

Below: The Seaboard Air Line was actually a railroad, and it eventually called itself the Seaboard Air Line Railroad. Many people, however, remember it for the nickname 'Route of the Silver Fleet.' Among that fleet, there were such classics as the *Silver Star*, *Silver Comet*, and the great *Silver Meteor* seen here, circa 1939.

Bottom: The Seaboard's greatest train, however, was none other than the *Orange Blossom Special*, seen here headed south in 1922.

Centrale. Paralleling the *Adirondack* today, and running as far south as Washington, is the *Montrealer*. It follows the old Mohawk Trail, while the *Adirondack* follows the Hudson.

Other names were deliberately chosen to capture a particular mood or a specific clientele. One can imagine how the club car chatter turned to finance on the New York, New Haven & Hartford's *Bankers*, that great Springfield to Washington, DC, streamliner. Knowing exactly what went on in its plush club cars, the New York, New Haven & Hartford also ran a *Cigar Valley Express* between New York and Springfield. Running from Washington, DC, to Elsworth, Maine (hard by Bar Harbor), via New York and Portland, the *Bar Harbor Express* was operated jointly by the Maine Central, the Boston & Maine and the New York, New Haven & Hartford. The latter was, however, the key operator.

Gliding through the picturesque Appalachian region that was its namesake, the *Blue Ridge* was the classic service between Washington, DC, and Martinsburg, West Virginia. The Norfolk & Western can be recalled for its *Pelican* (New York to New Orleans), its *Pocahontas* (Norfolk to Chicago) and its *Birmingham Special* (New York to Birmingham via Washington and Chattanooga). However, the greatest of the Norfolk & Western streamliners were the marvelous *Powhatan Arrow* (Norfolk to Cincinnati) and the *Tennessean* (New York to Memphis in cooperation with the Pennsylvania Railroad).

Fabled in song like few other trains, the *Orange Blossom Special* was operated by the Pennsylvania Railroad south from New York, by the Richmond, Fredericksburg & Potomac in the Middle Atlantic and by the Seaboard Air Line railroad from Richmond to Miami. A sister train to the legendary *Orange Blossom Special*, the *Silver Meteor* traversed the busy New York to Miami run under the auspices of three railroads. The Pennsylvania took her south out of New York, turned her over to the Richmond, Fredericksburg & Potomac, which took her into Richmond, where the Seaboard Air Line assumed control for the remainder of the trip. Today, Amtrak's *Silver Meteor* operates between New York and Miami over much of the same track as the classic version.

Although the great streamliners are all gone, it is still possible to travel the same routes and capture a hint of the old magic by virtue of the fact that Amtrak has retained some of the old names. The eastern seaboard is particularly rich in this form of nostalgia. One can still travel south from Montreal on the *Adirondack* to New York or the *Montrealer* all the way to Washington. South from New York, one can choose from a menu that brings nostalgic tears to a passenger train buff's eyes. There is the *Virginian* to Washington; the *Old Dominion* to Newport News; the *Carolinian* to Charlotte; the *Palmetto* to Jacksonville; the *Silver Star* to St Petersburg and Miami via Columbia; and the classic *Silver Meteor* to St Petersburg and Miami via Charleston.

SEABOARD AIR LINE RAILROAD — THROUGH THE HEART OF THE SOUTH

Seaboard AIR LINE RAILROAD
ROUTE OF THE ORANGE BLOSSOM SPECIAL

EQUIPMENT OF THROUGH TRAINS BETWEEN EASTERN CITIES AND FLORIDA, ATLANTA, BIRMINGHAM AND THE SOUTHWEST.

SOUTHBOUND

THE SILVER METEOR—No. 57-157.
(Coach Seats Reserved.)

Baggage Dormitory Car	New York to Miami.
Reclining Seat Coach (52 Seats)..11-E	New York to Miami.
10-Roomette, 6-D.B.R........S-101	New York to Miami.
10 Roomette, 6-D.B.R...S-102, S-103	New York to Miami.
6-D.B.R., Buffet Lounge.....S-104	New York to Miami.
Reclining Seat P. & B. Car	Wildwood to St. Petersburg.
10 Roomette, 6-D.B.R........S-105	New York to Sarasota-Venice.
10-Roomette, 6-D.B.R..S-106, S-107	New York to St. Petersburg.
SAL Dining Car	New York to St. Petersburg.
Reclining Seat Coaches (52 Seats)..18-W, 19-W	N. Y. to St. Petersburg.
Reclining Seat Coach	Tampa to Sarasota-Venice (seats not reserved).
SAL Dining Car	New York to Miami.
Reclining Seat Coaches (52 Seats)..12-E, 13-E, 14-E	New York to Miami.
Tavern Observation Car	New York to Miami.

ORANGE BLOSSOM SPECIAL—No. 45.
(All Pullman.) (Last trip April 11.)

Baggage Dormitory Car	New York to Miami.
6-Sec., 6-D.B.R........OB-20	New York to Miami.
12-Rmtte., 1-S.B.R., 4-D.B.R..OB-21	New York to Miami.
2-Cpt., 1-D.R., Buf. Lge....OB-22	New York to Miami.
SAL Dining Car	New York to Miami.
6-Cpt., 3-D.R........OB-23	New York to Miami.
6-Cpt., 3-D.R........OB-24	New York to Miami.
6-Cpt., 3-D.R........OB-25	New York to Miami.
6-Cpt., 3-D.R........OB-26	New York to Miami.
6-Cpt., 3-D.R........OB-28	New York to Miami.
8-Sec., 1-D.R., 3-D.B.R......MS-7	Boston to Miami. (Last trip April 4.)
SAL Dining Car	Washington to Wildwood.
6-Sec., 4-Romette, 4-D.B.R..R-361	Washington to Miami.
3-Cpt., 1-D.R., Buf. Lge.....R-362	Washington to Miami.

THE SILVER STAR—Nos. 21-121
(Coach Seats Reserved.)

Baggage Dormitory Car	New York to Miami.
10-Roomette, 6-D.B.R........S-109	New York to Miami.
8-Sec., 5-D.B.R........S-110	New York to Miami.
6-Cpt., Buf. Lge........S-111	New York to Miami.
6-Cpt., 3-D.R........S-112	New York to Port Boca Grande.
8-Sec., 5-D.B.R........S-113	New York to St. Petersburg.
10-Roomette, 6-D.B.R........S-114	New York to St. Petersburg.
SAL Dining Car	New York to St. Petersburg.
Reclining Seat Coaches (52 Seats)..7-W, 8-W	N. Y. to St. Petersburg.
SAL Dining Car	New York to Miami.
Tavern Coach (24 Recl. Seats)...2-E	New York to Miami.
Reclining Seat Coach (36 Seats)..3-E	New York to Miami.
Reclining Seat Coach (52 Seats)..4-E	New York to Miami.
Reclining Seat Coach (52 Seats)..5-E	New York to Miami.
Obs. Coach (40 Recl. Seats).....6-E	New York to Miami.

THE SILVER COMET—No. 33.
(Coach Seats Reserved.)

P. & B. Dormitory Car (14 Recl. Seats) 21-B	Washington to Birmingham.
Reclining Seat Coach (52 Seats) 22-B	New York to Birmingham.
Reclining Seat Coach (52 Seats).28-B	Portsmouth to Atlanta. (See Note.)
10-Sec., 1-D.R., 2-Cpt........B-3	Portsmouth to Atlanta. (See Note.)
10-Rmtte., 6-D.B.R........R-365	Washington to Atlanta.
10-Sec., 1-D.R., 2-Cpt........R-366	Washington to Birmingham.
10 Roomette, 6-D.B.R........S-119	New York to Birmingham.
10-Section, Lounge........S-120	New York to Birmingham.
SAL Dining Car	New York to Birmingham.
Reclining Seat Coaches (52 Seats)..23-B, 24-B	New York to Birmingham.
Tavern Observation	New York to Birmingham.

NOTE—Handled on Train 7 Norlina to Hamlet.

THE PALMLAND—No. 9-1.

Baggage Car	Washington to Miami.
Coaches (Two)	New York to Miami.
Coach	Tampa-West Lake Wales to Miami.
Passenger and Baggage Car	Jacksonville to Tampa.
Coach	New York to Tampa.
Coach	Tampa to Port Boca Grande.
SAL Parlor Dining Car	Tampa to Port Boca Grande.
SAL Dining Car	Raleigh to Jacksonville.
12-Rmtte., 1-S.B.R., 4-D.B.R..S-115	N. Y. to Southern Pines-Hamlet.
8-Sec., 1-D.R., 3-D.B.R.....S-116	N. Y. to Southern Pines-Hamlet.
10-Sec., 1-D.R., 2-Cpt........R-350	Washington to Hamlet.
8-Sec., 5-D.B.R........S-117	New York to Miami.
10-Sec., 1-D.R., 2-Cpt........4332	Cleveland-Jacksonville to Tampa.
10-Sec., 1-D.R., 2-Cpt........CS-2	Tampa-West Lake Wales to Miami.

NORTHBOUND

THE SILVER METEOR—No. 158-58.
(Coach Seats Reserved.)

Baggage Dormitory Car	Miami to New York.
Reclining Seat Coach (52 Seats) 11-E	Miami to New York.
10-Roomette, 6-D.B.R..B-50, B-51, B-52	Miami to New York.
6-D.B.R., Buffet Lounge.....B-53	Miami to New York.
Reclining Seat P. & B. Car	St. Petersburg to Wildwood.
10 Roomette, 6-D.B.R........B-48	Venice-Sarasota to New York.
10-Roomette, 6-D.B.R....B-58, B-59	St. Petersburg to New York.
SAL Dining Car	St. Petersburg to New York.
Reclining Seat Coaches (52 Seats)..18-W, 19-W	St. Petersburg to N. Y.
Reclining Seat Coach	Venice-Sarasota to Tampa (seats not reserved).
SAL Dining Car	Miami to New York.
Reclining Seat Coaches (52 Seats)..12-E, 13-E, 14-E	Miami to New York.
Tavern Observation Car	Miami to New York.

ORANGE BLOSSOM SPECIAL—No. 46.
(All Pullman.) (Last trip April 13.)

Baggage Dormitory Car	Miami to New York.
6-Sec., 6-D.B.R........B-20	Miami to New York.
12-Rmtte., 1-S.B.R., 4-D.B.R..B-21	Miami to New York.
2-Cpt., 1-D.R., Buf. Lge......B-22	Miami to New York.
SAL Dining Car	Miami to New York.
6-Cpt., 3-D.R..B-23, B-24, B-25, B-26, B-28	Miami to New York.
8-Sec., 1-D.R., 3-D.B.R......B-29	Miami to Boston. (Last trip April 6.)
SAL Dining Car	Wildwood to Washington.
6-Sec., 4-Roomette, 4-D.B.R..B-30	Miami to Washington.
3-Cpt., 1-D.R., Buf. Lge.....B-27	Miami to Washington.

THE SILVER STAR—Nos. 122-22.
(Coach Seats Reserved.)

Baggage Dormitory Car	Miami to New York.
10-Roomette, 6-D.B.R........B-45	Miami to New York.
8-Sec., 5-D.B.R........B-46	Miami to New York.
6-Cpt., Buffet Lounge........B-47	Miami to New York.
6-Cpt., 3-D.R........B-55	Port Boca Grande to New York.
8-Sec., 5-D.B.R........B-56	St. Petersburg to New York.
10-Roomette, 6-D.B.R........B-57	St. Petersburg to New York.
SAL Dining Car	St. Petersburg to New York.
Reclining Seat Coaches (52 Seats)..7-W, 8-W	St. Petersburg to N.Y.
SAL Dining Car	Miami to New York.
Tavern Coach (24 Recl. Seats)...2-E	Miami to New York.
Reclining Seat Coach (36 Seats)..3-E	Miami to New York.
Reclining Seat Coaches (52 Seats)..4-E, 5-E	Miami to New York.
Obs. Coach (40 Recl. Seats).....6-E	Miami to New York.

THE SILVER COMET—No. 34.
(Coach Seats Reserved.)

P. & B. Dormitory Car (14 Recl. Seats)..21-B	Birmingham to Washington.
Reclining Seat Coach (52 Seats).22-B	Birmingham to New York.
Reclining Seat Coach (52 Seats).28-B	Atlanta to Portsmouth. (See Note.)
10-Sec., 1-D.R., 2-Cpt........B-4	Atlanta to Portsmouth. (See Note.)
10-Roomette, 6-D.B.R........B-70	Atlanta to Washington.
10-Sec., 1-D.R., 2-Cpt........B-71	Birmingham to Washington.
10 Roomette, 6-D.B.R........B-72	Birmingham to New York.
10-Section, Lounge........B-74	Birmingham to New York.
SAL Dining Car	Birmingham to New York.
Reclining Seat Coaches (52 Seats)..23-B, 24-B	Birmingham to New York.
Tavern Observation	Birmingham to New York.

NOTE—Handled on Train 8 Hamlet to Norlina.

THE PALMLAND—No. 2-10.

Baggage Car	Miami to New York.
Coaches (Two)	Miami to New York.
Coach	Miami to West Lake Wales-Tampa.
Passenger and Baggage Car	Tampa to Jacksonville.
Coach	Tampa to New York.
Coach	Port Boca Grande to Tampa.
SAL Parlor Dining Car	Port Boca Grande to Tampa.
Dining Car (Lounge)	Washington to New York.
SAL Dining Car	Jacksonville to Raleigh.
8-Sec., 1-D.R., 3-D.B.R.......B-63	Hamlet-Southern Pines to N. Y.
12-Rmtte., 1-S.B.R., 4-D.B.R...B-64	Hamlet-Southern Pines to N. Y.
10-Sec., 1-D.R., 2-Cpt........B-91	Hamlet to Washington.
8-Sec., 5-D.B.R........B-122	Miami to New York.
10-Sec., 1 D.R., 2-Cpt........B-123	Tampa to Jacksonville-Cleveland.
10-Sec., 1-DR., 2-Cpt........CS-2	Miami to West Lake Wales-Tampa.

ROUTES WEST OF CHICAGO

By the beginning of the twentieth century, there were several transcontinental railroads and, upon them, many great trains that made the run all the way from Chicago to the Pacific. Meanwhile others served the growing network of rail lines in the upper Midwest.

Archetypal of the classic trains west of Chicago were the Chicago, Burlington & Quincy *Zephyrs*. The word itself—melodious, yet mysterious—captured the mood of the great West and of the train, having been derived from the Latin *zephyr*, meaning 'west wind.' Looking west from Council

Bluffs, Iowa, on his famous visit in 1858, Abraham Lincoln beheld the vastness of North America's Great Plains and felt the *zephyr* blow against the chiseled features of his face. He envisioned a great railroad that could one day bring the two coasts together by spanning this expanse before him. This led to Lincoln's championing of what became the Pacific Railroad Act of 1862, which led in turn to the completion of a transcontinental railroad when the rails of the Central Pacific and the Union Pacific railroads met at Promontory, Utah, in May 1869.

The Chicago, Burlington & Quincy named its early fast diesel trains *Zephyrs*. Most were destination-named, such as the *California Zephyr*, *Denver Zephyr*, *Texas Zephyr*, *Twin Cities Zephyr* and the *Nebraska Zephyr*, but among them there was a *Mark Twain Zephyr*.

The Fort Worth & Denver line had a *Sam Houston Zephyr*, a combination that would perhaps have puzzled the craggy old fighter of San Jacinto. The *Silver Streak Zephyr*, serving Kansas City, Omaha and Lincoln, was named for the appearance of the train itself.

Today, Amtrak operates a *California Zephyr* over the same route as one of its three primary routes between Chicago and the West Coast. It provides a 20-hour service between Chicago and Salt Lake City, where it intersects with Amtrak's *Pioneer* (to Portland) and *Desert Wind* (to Los Angeles), before continuing a 16-hour run over Southern Pacific track to Oakland.

On 26 May 1934, a three-car, articulated streamliner sped a thousand miles from Denver, Colorado, to Chicago, Illinois, in 14 hours in a dawn-to-dusk, non-stop run that was to officially open the second year of Chicago's great 'Century of Progress Exposition.' This famous trip culminated at the 'Wings of a Century' pageant on Chicago's lakefront, where at 8:09 pm the *Pioneer Zephyr* rolled onto the stage. Its run had set a world long-distance record and had firmly established the value of diesel-electric power. The applause of the World's Fair goers only added to the acclaim this unique train had received at every town along the Burlington's right-of-way. Thus, the *Pioneer Zephyr*—the first diesel streamliner—ushered in a new era in rail transportation. In the brief 14 hours of its spectacular run it had dramatized the application of the internal combustion engine in main line railroad service and indicated the practicability of the two-cycle diesel engine in rail service.

The *Pioneer Zephyr* convinced the railroads that the diesel engine had an important future in railroad power. The prototype engines were built by the Electro-Motive Company, founded in 1922 and a subsidiary of General Motors since 1930. Their diesel engines were used in 1933 to provide power for the Chevrolet assembly line at the Chicago 'Century of Progress' Exposition. Although at the time they were strictly experimental and difficult to keep running, the engines attracted the attention of Burlington president Ralph Budd, who was then contracting with the Budd Company in Philadelphia to build the small, three-car *Zephyr* train. He needed a prime mover for the revolutionary new train and met with Charles Kettering at General Motors. Budd finally persuaded Kettering to

Below: **When the Burlington's *Pioneer Zephyr* made her inaugural run in 1934, America's first diesel was unlike anything that had gone before. She was a glittering steel gem of classic machine age splendor. She captured the imagination of her era and spawned a whole family of trains that would adopt her surname.**

make one of the new engines available for the *Zephyr*. He later remarked that while Kettering expressed qualms about the feasibility of using such an experimental prime mover before it had been thoroughly tested in the laboratory, he and his Chicago, Burlington & Quincy associates had no fears because once Kettering had committed himself, he'd have to stand behind his decision. Subsequent events proved Budd right and sowed the seeds for the tremendous locomotive power development which, over the next two decades, would see the end of steam power, the force that had dominated American railroad service for the preceding 100 years. In reporting the maiden run of the *Pioneer Zephyr* to his directors on the Burlington board, Budd emphasized two facts: the fuel cost for the 1000-mile trip was $14.64, and the highest speed attained was 112.5 mph. In a nutshell, he was highlighting economy and speed, the basis for the coming revolution in railroading.

Buoyed by the success of the *Pioneer Zephyr*—the continent's first diesel streamliner—Burlington spawned a whole family of *Zephyrs*.

The classic *California Zephyr* originally was operated between Chicago and San Francisco by a consortium of railroads led by the Chicago, Burlington & Quincy. The *California Zephyr*, spectacularly streamlined with five Vista-Domes, was jointly owned and operated by the Burlington, Rio Grande and Western Pacific railroads. The *California Zephyr* route involved the Burlington as far as the Dotsero cutoff in Colorado, whereupon the train operated under Denver & Rio Grande and Western Pacific motive power into San Francisco. The first Chicago to San Francisco 'Zephyr' actually was the *Exposition Flyer*, started in 1939, but which was renamed in 1949, when it became a Vista-Dome streamliner.

Particularly in the Rocky Mountains, the views from the classic trains were spectacular. It was because of this fact that the idea of the modern observation dome was conceived on a July day in 1944, by CR Osborn, vice president of General Motors. Riding in the glass nose of a diesel, it struck him that a glass-topped passenger car would be popular. It was just a year later when the first Vista-Dome went into service on the Chicago, Burlington & Quincy, and today a monument still stands beside the tracks where Mr Osborn had his idea.

Vista-Domes were particularly applicable to trains traveling through the spectacular scenery of the mountain West. Soon after World War II ended in 1945, trains like the *California Zephyr* mentioned above, the *Denver Zephyr*, the *Rio Grande Zephyr*, the *Western Star* and the *Royal Gorge* sported a Vista-Dome.

When the passenger went to sleep that night aboard a train such as the *Royal Gorge*, a pale moon glimmered on the tumbling Colorado River, flowing west to Boulder Dam and the Gulf of California. When he awakened he was on the roof of the continent, Tennessee Pass, 10,240 feet high, and sunrise pinkened an eastbound river, the Arkansas, headed for the Mississippi. As the passenger breakfasted, breathless vistas unfolded

Above: **The Burlington ran the *California Zephyr* out of Chicago, but by the time she reached the Feather River Canyon (seen here), where the Vista-Dome was 'standing room only,' she was in the capable hands of the Western Pacific.**

at every turn of the wheels. Far to the south, the snowy minarets of the Sangre de Cristo range were scarlet in the early light, just as Spanish explorers first saw them and named them Blood of Christ.

Then, in midmorning, the train dipped into the big thrill of this route for which the train is named—the mystic Royal Gorge. The Vista-Dome was the place to enjoy it. The brightly colored canyon walls closed in, soaring until they seemed almost to meet half a mile straight up, and the floor of the gorge was bathed in an eerie, rose-tinted shadow. Where the train stopped, a traveler could flip pebbles from one wall to the other. A fifth of a mile overhead, a dark thread against the sky marked an

engineering marvel, the world's highest highway bridge. East of the gorge passengers began to catch distant glimpses of Pike's Peak, the most famous of the Rocky Mountains (although 27 are higher), and it was still visible when the *Royal Gorge* pulled into Denver.

During the golden age of rail travel in the 1950s, the *California Zephyr* plied the rails between Chicago and Oakland, with a through sleeper to New York. Seated in this train's sunny Vista-Dome, passengers had a commanding view of the countryside as it rolled past. In the early afternoon, the *California Zephyr* bored into one of the far West's wonderlands, the Feather River Canyon, for the long ascent up the Sierra Nevada. Wholly un-

like travel in a regular car, the Vista-Dome accessed scenery not only to the sides and the front and rear, but also allowed viewing upward, and gave passengers a panorama that made them feel as if they were truly amidst the wonders that they viewed.

The *California Zephyr*'s Vista-Dome revealed the famous canyon in all its majesty—the frothing river beside the tracks, the lofty evergreen slopes and craggy ramparts soaring to the blue wedge of sky far above. Passengers might also have noticed a peculiar, fence-like string of wires beside the tracks and asked what it was. A helpful steward would be glad to answer that it was a landslide detector. Any falling rocks would break one of the detector's wires before reaching the rails and every train would stop automatically until the line was inspected and cleared.

The recorded musical programs over the public address system during the day had been interrupted occasionally by a pleasant voice announcing sights of interest. Later, the traveler might chance to meet the person behind the voice, the so-called 'Zephyrette,' a service employee whose job was similar to that of an airline stewardess.

At bedtime, the passenger would become better acquainted with his or her roomette, a compact, private room. Already made up, the bed was hidden in the wall. It was lowered with a flick of the

Below: The Union Pacific's *City of Los Angeles* at Echo Canyon in 1955. The Union Pacific operated a fleet of 'Cities,' including the *City of St Louis*, the *City of Portland*, the *City of Denver*, and the *City of San Francisco*, which was operated in cooperation with Chicago & NorthWestern and the Southern Pacific, which actually took her into her namesake via the Oakland Pier.

wrist, and the piped-in music was equally easily turned down, so that the passenger could fall asleep, or raise the window shade and watch the lights of automobiles racing across the Nevada desert.

West of Chicago, particularly in the Midwest and Upper Plains, Native American names—both those of tribes and chiefs—were immortalized in the names of many trains. The most famous was the Milwaukee Road's fleet of *Hiawathas*. The Chicago & North Western had a *Mondamin*, while the Norfolk & Western had the *Pocahontas* and *Powhatan Arrow*, and the Chicago, Burlington & Quincy had the *Black Hawk*.

As for the tribes, the Missouri Pacific ran the *Aztec Eagle* into Mexico, and the Rock Island ran the *Cherokee Imperial* to Los Angeles and the *Choctaw Rocket* to Oklahoma. The Milwaukee had the *Chippewa Hiawatha* and the *Sioux*. The Illinois Central had the *Chickasaw*, and with the Georgia Central, the *Seminole*. In the east, the New York Central operated the *Iroquois* and the *Tuscarora*, while Southern Pacific of Mexico had *El Yaqui*. Of course, New England rails had many old, well-known names like *Narragansett*,

Kennebec, *Penobscot* and *Katahdin*, and the New York, New Haven & Hartford, with a playful liking for tongue twisters, added the *Umpechanee*, the *Mahkeenac* and the *Mahawie*.

Few regions in the United States had better train service during rail travel's halcyon century than the stretch between Chicago and the Twin Cities of Minneapolis and St Paul, Minnesota. Streamliners once raced one another back and forth all around the clock. The passenger traveling this route had the option to select a train with a magnificent observation car such as one of several trains known as the *Hiawatha*. Among these were the Chicago to Minneapolis *Morning Hiawatha* and its sister train, the *Afternoon Hiawatha*, as well as the Chicago to Sioux Falls *Midwest Hiawatha*, the Milwaukee to Ontanagon *Chippewa Hiawatha* and the Chicago to Minneapolis *Twin Cities Hiawatha*.

The *Olympian Hiawatha* was the most ambitious, running from the Milwaukee hub to Minneapolis and then to Seattle and Tacoma. It had an economy-priced sleeper called *Touralux*, a streamlined version of the old-time tourist car. Another innovation was a spacious rear-end, glass-domed observation section called a Skytop Lounge. The highlight of the train, however, was its observation car, called a Super-Dome, twice the size of most such cars, with 68 seats upstairs over an elegant lounge-cafe. Each window of the immense dome cost the Milwaukee Road $400, and the two Super-Dome cars cost half a million dollars, a lot of money in the late 1940s. The train itself cost $1.5 million.

As the *Hiawathas* rolled past Milwaukee's lovely parks and on past lakes with such names as Pewaulkee, Nagawicka and Okauchee, the bartender in the Super-Dome lounge would regale interested passengers with the finest beverages—from liqueurs to fruit juice and soft drinks.

Today, Amtrak maintains an elaborate schedule of more than half a dozen Chicago-centered routes that it calls its 'Hiawatha Service.' These *Hiawathas* serve Milwaukee and Chicago with trains every three hours throughout most of the day.

The trains operated by the Chicago, Rock Island & Pacific were known generally as the *Rocket*s, which in its passenger cars, memorialized its own mountain area with cars named *Grand Mesa* and *Garden of the Gods*. The

Rockets were a family of streamliners known formally as the '*Rock Island Rockets*,' or the '*Rocket Fleet*.' They included the *Choctaw Rocket*, which ran between Memphis and Oklahoma City; the *Corn Belt Rocket*, which ran between Chicago and Omaha; the *Des Moines Rocket*, which ran between Chicago and Des Moines; the *Peoria Rocket*, which ran between Chicago and Peoria; the *Quad City Rocket*, which ran between Chicago and Rock Island; the *Rocky Mountain Rocket*, which ran between Chicago, Denver and Colorado Springs; the *Twin Star Rocket*, which connected Minneapolis, St Paul, Kansas City and Houston; and the *Zephyr Rocket*, which linked Minneapolis, St Paul and St Louis.

To promote its celebrated *Rockets*, Rock Island's public relations department wrote a prose poem about a young girl gazing wistfully at a passing *Rocket*: 'Most any afternoon you can see her there ... wistful eyes following the trim lines of a diesel-powered *Rock Island Rocket*. Smoothly, quietly it speeds westward to distant cities and regions of enchantment. They're dream places to her now, but there will come a day when this young lady will board a *Rocket* ... and then her dream places will become happy realities. And she will experience the pleasure of train travel as fine as it's possible to make it!'

One of America's greatest railroads, the Atchison, Topeka & Santa Fe, created

Above: **The Chicago, Rock Island & Pacific—known universally as the Rock Island Line—operated a fleet of classic trains with the surname 'Rocket' which were known collectively as the 'Rock Island *Rockets*.' There wasn't a *Rocket* named for every destination in the upper Midwest, but it seemed like it, and many of them could actually take you to Rock Island.**

Opposite bottom: **The Rock Island Line's *Rocky Mountain Rocket* left Chicago around breakfast time, got you into Denver the following evening, and to Colorado Springs just after midnight.**

Opposite top: **Just as the Rock Island had its fabled *Rocket* fleet, the Milwaukee Road had its classic family of *Hiawatha*s. The *Olympian Hiawatha* was the queen, but there were also a *Morning* and an *Afternoon Hiawatha* to choose from between Chicago and Minneapolis.**

62

The **Chief** is still the Chief

Santa Fe

America's New Railroad

Now—only 39½ hours Chicago-Los Angeles...Only one night en route westbound...Extra fare dropped...Reserved seat chair cars...Same fine Pullman accommodations...Fred Harvey food—from full-course menus to low-cost budget meals.

Also...*Super Chief extra fare now only $7.50 on this all-private-room streamliner, Chicago-Los Angeles.*
El Capitan extra fare dropped on this only all-chair-car streamliner, Chicago-Los Angeles.

Above: The *Super Chief* was indeed the 'chief,' the most glorious of Santa Fe—and possibly of all Western—trains. Actually the point of this late-1950s advertising was to say that taking the train was better than driving. This was a sign of the times, but historically intriguing because the highway that parallelled the run of the *Super Chief* was none other than US Route 66, the main street of American dreams.

Today in Amtrack colors, the *Chief* is the *Southwest Chief*, and takes 48 hours to make the run.

a standard for passenger train service that few other American railroads could match. For example, the Santa Fe's *Super Chief* easily matched the quality of the New York Central's *Twentieth Century Limited*—a train that was synonymous with luxury and prestige.

The *Super Chief* became famous for its luxurious appointments and excellent food and, in the 1940s and 1950s, it was the train ridden by the rich and famous.

While the Santa Fe was not the first railroad to use diesels for passenger service, it was the first to take advantage of diesel power plants for streamlined passenger service from the Midwest to the West Coast.

Although extremely experimental, diesels already attracted the attention of the Burlington Railroad, which was seeking a revolutionary new train to attract passengers lost to the automobile. As noted above, Burlington persuaded Gen-

eral Motors to make one of the engines available for its new train. Despite reluctance on the part of General Motors, the engine and the experimental train proved successful and the age of the diesel locomotive was born.

The *Super Chief* soon became one of the best-known passenger trains in the world, was used extensively by Hollywood motion picture stars and other celebrities. It had succeeded the *Chief*, an all-steam train that ran between the Chicago and Los Angeles beginning in 1923. The all-Pullman *Super Chief* was followed by *El Capitan*, an all-coach streamlined diesel train inaugurated between Los Angeles and Chicago in 1938.

Soon after the introduction of diesels in the 1930s, the fastest runs in the United States for both freight and passenger service were achieved by the new locomotives, and the days of steam locomotives were numbered. By 1943, two Santa Fe operating divisions were completely diesel, and by 1959 the last steam locomotives had been retired from the fleet.

Welcome to the
Turquoise Room

the only private dining room in the world on rails

aboard the new **Super Chief**

TURQUOISE ROOM · Santa Fe

Entertain in the grand manner while en route between Chicago and Los Angeles — in a perfectly appointed private dining room for a party up to ten.

The Turquoise Room in the new Lounge Car of the new Super Chief is the most distinctive social feature ever provided on any train.

You are invited to enjoy it, and the other new features on the beautiful new all-room Super Chief. For Turquoise Room reservations, just consult any Santa Fe ticket agent, or the dining-car steward on the Super Chief

R. T. Anderson, General Passenger Traffic Manager, Santa Fe System Lines, Chicago 4, Illinois

When the diesel proved its value in passenger service, Santa Fe officials set about replacing its freight service fleet of steam locomotives. The Electro-Motive Corporation delivered a 5400-horsepower engine to the Atchison, Topeka & Santa Fe in 1938. It was called *The Jeep*, which was given the number 100. *The Jeep* hauled its first train of 68 freight cars from Kansas City to Los Angeles under regular operating conditions, and proved that it could haul more freight cars up a grade at a higher speed than any steam locomotive in service at the time. Number 100 trimmed the time it took a freight train to traverse the distance from Chicago to Los Angeles from six to four days and then three days. In 1938, hauling a train from the Great Lakes to the West Coast by steam required nine engines and a total of 35 stops for fuel and water. Number 100, on the other hand, required just five stops.

Diesel power plants were unique. Instead of a single big steam plant, each diesel unit held four 900-horsepower diesel motors which generated current to drive eight traction motors, which were directly connected to the truck axles. If problems developed in one of the two diesel units, the other unit would continue to produce power, allowing the diesels to run continuously for long periods without major delays. On the other hand, if steam engines experienced trouble they were forced to shut down, and sometimes entire trains had to be halted until repairs could be made.

In addition, steam locomotives were available for just one-third of their operating lives, with the other two-thirds spent in repairs (although many roundhouse mechanics managed to keep some steam locomotives operating 60 percent of the time). Diesels, however, could be in service 95 percent of the time. The first diesels did not have quite the charm of the Santa Fe's *De Luxe*, a six-car steam passenger train that carried 70 passengers on its first run in 1911. This

Above: During the 1950s, in the last glorious days of the classic American trains, several roads made a point of elevating service above and beyond anything that had ever boon seen before, or since, in commercial rail travel. The Turquoise Room was unique, for after all, the 'new' *Super Chief* was indeed the 'chief.'

Above left: Santa Fe's classic *El Capitan* pulls into Albuquerque, New Mexico. The advertising used to promote Santa Fe's passenger routes to Los Angeles implied direct contact with the native peoples of the Southwest, but in fact, the only such contact took place during a brief whistle-stop in Albuquerque.

train featured two drawing room cars, an observation car, a dining car and a club car, as well as showers, bathtubs, electric hair-styling irons and an on-board library. Its crew included a ladies' maid, a barber, a manicurist and a hairdresser. The extra fare to take advantage of this service was $25, and the *De Luxe* took 63 hours to make the Chicago to Los Angeles run.

Not all Santa Fe passenger accommodations, however, were so luxurious as to prohibit the everyday American from using them. The Santa Fe, beginning in 1905, had offered a 'tourist class' sleeping car at reduced rates. They went from Chicago to California just as fast as the first-class Pullmans (they were usually part of the same train), stopped at the same Harvey Houses and passed through the same scenery. They even had a small 'baker oven' built onto the car's hot water heater. All they lacked were the plush upholstery and elaborately carved woodwork of the first-class cars.

Even without these luxuries, tourist class cars were immeasurably more pleasant than the 'immigrant trains,' which offered only wooden benches for their passengers. (Bedding was supplied by the sleeper.) As a result, tourist class accommodations were very popular with middle-class travelers—once the

Santa Fe was able to convince its customers that riding in tourist class was a respectable thing to do.

The original *Super Chief* featured two twin-diesel locomotives built by the Electro-Motive Corporation, (now the Electro-Motive Division of General Motors) at La Grange, Illinois. The locomotives, each rated at 3600 horsepower, were constructed in two units and were tested in different terrain and conditions before they were delivered to the Santa Fe. When the twin locomotives were put to the test hauling a nine-car Pullman, they broke the record set in 1905 by the Santa Fe steam locomotive *Coyote Special.*

With the test complete, the results were conclusive—diesel locomotives were here to stay. All that was needed was a sturdier track bed to support the high-flyer passenger train. Santa Fe spent $4 million improving the tracks and the roadbed between Los Angeles and Chicago before putting the *Super Chief* into daily service.

The diesel engines of the two locomotives proved they were better than steam engines and could operate at higher speeds for longer distances without expensive water stops along the way. Such water stops were required by steam locomotives, especially in desert climates.

The entire train was constructed of stainless steel, with sleepers from the Pullman Company and with club, baggage, dining and lounge cars constructed by the Budd Company. The cars were named after the Indian pueblos: *Isleta, Laguna, Acoma, Cochiti, Oriabi, Taos* and *Navajo*. The Santa Fe had an extensive list of cars named for Native Americans of the southwestern states, including *Betahtakin, Biltabito, Seboyeta, Hualpai, Jadito, Otowi, Kaibito, Moencopi, Nankoweap, Puye, Salahkai, Saydatoh, Tsankawi* and *Chimayo*. With a full passenger manifest, the train carried 104 people, not including the train crew and eight postal clerks. A second *Super Chief* unit also featured nine cars, giving Santa Fe twice-a-week service between Chicago and the West Coast. In the later 1930s, five-car trains were added to the streamliner service, giving Santa Fe 13 streamliners, more than any other railroad in the United States.

Many railroads, including the Santa Fe, prided themselves on their dining car service—even though most dining cars lost money. They were operated as loss leaders, with the expectation that excellent food and service would draw passengers from competing lines. The theory worked to the advantage of the Santa Fe and the Fred Harvey Company which operated their famous chain of Harvey House restaurants along the Santa Fe route. The Santa Fe made money on its passenger runs with reliable service and good food.

Though overshadowed by the *Super Chief*, the Santa Fe offered other trains such as the *Grand Canyon*, another Chicago to Los Angeles classic which had a cut-off that could actually take you to the Grand Canyon itself.

The Santa Fe also tried to cooperate with early airlines. In 1929, the railroad pioneered cross-country service via the New York Central and Universal Air Lines, as well as with the Pennsylvania Railroad and Transcontinental Air Transport. Passengers boarded a train in New York, then took an airplane from Chicago to New Mexico. There they boarded a Santa Fe train bound for Los Angeles. The trip took three nights and two days. The service continued long enough for better passenger planes to come into service, thus rendering the train connections obsolete. Throughout the early days of railroading, few improvements had been made to dining cars. George Pullman had taken out the original patents in 1865 for cars in which passengers could sit and eat, but it was not until 1925 that the Santa Fe put its own design in service in hopes of creating an advantage over its rail competitors. A two-car set placed at the front of passenger trains included a diner and club lounger with a bath, barber shop and soda fountain, and held 42 customers in the diner alone. The trains also featured sleeping and shower facilities for the crew. The Santa Fe established a reputation for fast, reliable and comfortable passenger service long before the arrival of the *Super Chief*. For example, the Santa Fe's Edward Ripley was given credit for establishing the *California Limited*, which was for years one of the best known trains from the Midwest to the West Coast. It was an all-Pullman train, and all passengers had to purchase tickets. No free passes were allowed, not even for Ripley. Whenever he rode the train, he presented his ticket to the conductor just like the other passengers.

The *Limited* was extremely popular in the summer months when people were headed to and from California. Every day

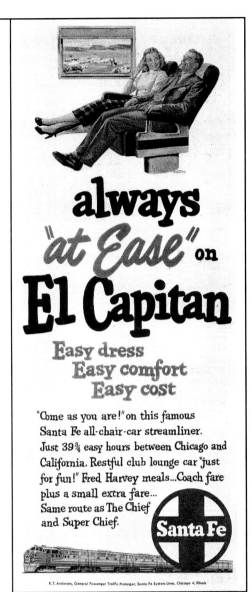

Above: While the *Super Chief* provided more upscale accommodations, *El Capitan* promoted the advantages of an 'all-chair-car streamliner.' The first 10 or 12 hours were fine, but sleeping in an 'all-chair-car streamliner' was like sleeping on an airplane. Nevertheless, it was a great way to meet new friends.

Facing page: The much-heralded *Super Chief* climbs the steep grade near the old Dick Wooton Ranch near Wooton, Colorado.

Below: **The classic Great Northern**
***Empire Builder* crosses the Continental Divide at Marias Pass, Montana, circa 1947.**

Opposite: **A contemporary view of Amtrak's *Empire Builder* nearing the Continental Divide at Marias Pass. It is here that the route follows the border of Glacier National Park, the crown jewel of Great Northern passenger advertising in the half century before 1970.**

as many as seven trains, each containing 11 sleeping cars filled with passengers, left Dearborn Station in Chicago or Union Station in Los Angeles within a half hour of each other. At one point, no fewer than 45 trains operated between the two cities.

The 45 trains—22 eastbound and 23 westbound—operated over the tracks simultaneously. During the three-day run, each train used a minimum of 15 locomotives with 15 train crews. For more than 10 years until the arrival of the *Super Chief*, the *California Limited* was the most popular train in the Santa Fe system.

Today, Amtrak operates its *Southwest Chief* over the same slice of Santa Fe trackage plied by the *Super Chief*—and the *Chief*—concluding the 2246-mile Chicago to Los Angeles service in 39 hours.

The Great Northern system was traditionally known as 'The route of the Empire Builder.' The basis of this title is dual, for it pays tribute to the memory and achievements of its founder, James Jerome 'Jim' Hill, and also distinguishes the line's principal passenger train, which traversed the immense territory to which Hill had devoted his life. The *Empire Builder*, the premier transcontinental passenger train of the Great

Northern Railway, began daily service—
with steam locomotives—between Chicago and the Pacific Coast in 1929, soon after the completion of the Cascade tunnel.

Great Northern's galaxy of streamlined trains began to take form in 1944 with the wartime announcement that five completely new *Empire Builders* would go into service between Chicago and the Pacific Northwest 'as soon as they could be assembled.' On 23 February 1947 these streamliners, each having 12 cars and a 4000-horsepower, two-unit, diesel-electric locomotive, began daily service. With the *Empire Builder*'s 45-

GREAT NORTHERN
EMPIRE BUILDER • WESTERN STAR—NEWEST AND BEST TO THE PACIFIC NORTHWEST

THE EMPIRE BUILDER

CHICAGO, ST. PAUL, MINNEAPOLIS, SPOKANE, SEATTLE AND PORTLAND with Direct Connections to and from TACOMA, BRITISH COLUMBIA AND CALIFORNIA
NO EXTRA FARE. ALL ACCOMMODATIONS RESERVED.

Daily No. 1—WEST			STATIONS.	EAST—No. 2 Daily	
Monday	1 00 P M	lve	Chicago (C.T.) C. B. & Q. arr.	2 00 P M	Wednesday
"	7 45 P M	arr	St. Paul C. B. & Q...lve.	7 15 A M	"
"	8 15 P M	lve	St. Paul G. N. Ry...arr.	7 00 A M	"
"	8 45 P M	lve	Minneapolis...arr.	6 30 A M	"
"	10 16 P M	lve	Willmar...arr.	4 37 A M	"
Tuesday	12 05 A M	lve	Breckenridge...arr.	2 25 A M	"
"	1 15 A M	lve	Fargo...lve.	1 20 A M	"
"	3 08 A M	lve	New Rockford...arr.	11 19 P M	Tuesday
"	4 50 A M	arr	Minot...lve.	9 40 P M	"
"	4 55 A M	arr	Minot...arr.	9 35 P M	"
"	7 20 A M	arr	Williston (C.T.)...lve.	7 10 P M	"
"	6 20 A M	lve	Williston (M.T.)...arr.	6 10 P M	"
"	b9 10 A M	lve	Glasgow...arr.	c3 20 P M	"
"	12 10 P M	arr	Havre...lve.	12 30 P M	"
Tuesday	3 45 P M	arr	Great Falls...lve.	9 00 A M	Tuesday
Tuesday	12 10 P M	lve	Havre...arr.	12 30 P M	Tuesday
"	2 10 P M	lve	Shelby...arr.	10 30 A M	"
"	a245 P M	arr	Cut Bank...lve.	d9 56 A M	"
"	6 15 P M	arr	Whitefish...lve.	6 40 A M	"
Tuesday	6 45 P M	arr	Kalispell (See Note▲)lve.	5 50 A M	Tuesday
Tuesday	6 15 P M	lve	Whitefish...arr.	6 40 A M	Tuesday
"	9 15 P M	lve	Troy (M.T.)...lve.	3 40 A M	"
"	8 15 P M	lve	Troy (P. T.)...arr.	2 40 A M	"
"	11 30 P M	arr	Spokane...lve.	11 15 P M	Monday
Wednesday	12 06 A M	lve	Spokane S.P. & S.Ry. arr.	10 35 P M	Monday
"	3 00 A M	lve	Pasco...lve.	7 35 P M	"
"	7 30 A M	arr	Portland...lve.	3 00 P M	"
Tuesday	11 59 P M	lve	Spokane G. N. Ry...arr.	10 45 P M	Monday
Wednesday	3 25 A M	arr	Wenatchee...lve.	7 15 P M	"
"	5 49 A M	arr	Skykomish...lve.	5 12 P M	"
"	7 02 A M	arr	Everett...lve.	3 55 P M	"
"	8 00 A M	arr	Seattle (King Street Station)..lve.	3 00 P M	"
Wednesday	*11 40 A M	arr	Vancouver...lve.	*12 30 P M	Monday
Wednesday	‡8 30 8 20	lve	Seattle (King Street Station)..arr.	‡1 45 2 00	Monday
"	9 04 —	arr	Auburn...lve.	1 04 —	"
"	‡9 15 —	arr	Puyallup...lve.	‡12 47 —	"
"	9 35 9 12	arr	Tacoma...lve.	12 30 1 05	Monday

EXPLANATION OF SIGNS.
a Stops to discharge revenue passengers from Williston and east and to pick up revenue passengers for Spokane and west where No. 1 is scheduled to stop; *b* stops to discharge revenue passengers from Minot, N.D., and east thereof and will stop on flag to receive revenue passengers for Spokane and west where No. 1 is scheduled to stop *c* stops on flag to discharge revenue passengers from Spokane and west and to pick up revenue passengers for Minot and east where No. 2 is scheduled to stop; *d* stops to discharge revenue passengers from Spokane and west and to pick up revenue passengers for Williston and east where No. 2 is scheduled to stop. *Connection made via Everett. ‡ Time shown is for Union Station. #Time shown is for North Puyallup. **Note ▲** — Bus service between Whitefish and Kalispell for passengers with through rail tickets.

LIGHTWEIGHT STREAMLINED EQUIPMENT.
Observation-Lounge Car between Chicago and Seattle. Buffet service and radio reception. Sleeper-Buffet-Lounge Car between Spokane and Portland via S. P. & S. Ry. (Contains Roomettes and Double Bedrooms, *Car 10 westbound, 20 eastbound*).
Standard Sleepers offering seven latest types of Pullman accommodations—Drawing-rooms, Compartments, Double Bedrooms, Roomettes, Duplex Roomettes, Lower and Upper Berths. Between Chicago and Seattle—four Sleepers (*14-15-16-17 westbound, 24-25-26-27 eastbound*).
Between Chicago and Portland—two Sleepers (11-12 *westbound*, 21-22 *eastbound*). (Via S. P. & S. Ry. between Spokane and Portland.)
Between Spokane and Portland—one Sleeper containing six Roomettes and three Double Bedrooms, Buffet-Lounge facilities. (*Westbound Car 10—ready for occupancy at Spokane at 9 30 p.m., eastbound Car 20.*) Via S. P. & S. Ry.
Advance reservations of Pullman accommodations on the "Empire Builder" may be made at any time prior to scheduled departure except as follows:
Pullman space on the "Empire Builder" for intermediate travel between any two stations west of Havre or between any two stations east of Havre may not be reserved until 24 hours prior to departure time eastbound from Seattle-Portland or westbound from Chicago.
Streamlined Day-Nite Coaches. Reclining seats with leg rests forming a couch for sleeping. Individual reading lights. Commodious lounge and dressing rooms—two lounges for women with curtained dressing alcoves. Radio reception. **All seats reserved in advance at no extra charge.** Seats also reserved for children under five years of age at no extra fare. (Pillows available.) **Passengers should be informed of the desirability of making advance coach seat reservations so that they may obtain definite coach seat assignments before their departure from originating point.**
Between Chicago and Seattle—three coaches, one 60 seat car for intermediate travel and two 48 seat cars for transcontinental travel (*100-101-102 westbound, 200-201-202 eastbound*).
Between Chicago and Seattle—one 48 seat coach (103 *westbound* 203 *eastbound*). Via S. P. & S. Ry. between Spokane and Portland.
Between Spokane and Portland, one 60 seat coach—(seats not reserved)—via S. P. & S. Ry.
The Ranch (Coffee Shop-Lounge Car). Lounge facilities for Coach and Pullman passengers. Radio reception. Coffee Shop with counter and table service at economical meal prices available throughout the day.
Dining Car with the most modern furnishings, decor and semi-private dining sections. Traditional Great Northern meals. To avoid standing in line for dinner, passengers have the choice of one-hour dining periods, beginning at 5 00 p.m. Passenger Representatives on the train arrange dinner reservations.
Tickets — All one-way and round-trip tickets will be honored on the Empire Builders (Nos. 1-2) except as follows: tickets endorsed Clergy, Charity, Employee, D. V. S., V. A. H., Blind and Attendant, Blind and Guide Dog, will not be honored. Circus, Show, Banana Messenger, Drover's or Caretaker's tickets and Live Stock Contracts will not be honored.
Baggage—Limited amount of checked baggage will be handled. Remains will not be handled **westbound** on train No. 1 between Chicago, St. Paul and Spokane.

hour schedule between Chicago in the East, and Seattle and Portland in the West, the Great Northern became the first northern transcontinental system to inaugurate streamliner service. These 1947 cars were the first completely new sleeper and coach transcontinental trains built in the nation after World War II ended, and the first since 1941, before the United States entered the conflict.

Another completely new fleet of five *Empire Builder* streamliners—the third generation under this name—entered service on 3 June 1951. Each had 15 cars and a 4500-horsepower, three-unit, diesel-electric locomotive. These trains,

again representing the most modern equipment and accommodations, took over the run and schedule of their predecessors. In the summer and early fall of 1955, four Vista-Dome cars—three dome coaches and a full-length dome lounge—all equipped with the ultimate in modern conveniences—were added to each of the five streamliners. During the summertime months of peak travel, the *Empire Builder* included 15 passenger cars, but that number was reduced during the winter months.

Also on 3 June 1951, the five *Empire Builder* streamliners that had begun operating in 1947 were joined by a sixth completely new train, the *Western Star*, which became the companion train of the *Empire Builder* on the Chicago to Seattle/Portland run. Thus, travelers on Great Northern's transcontinental line had their choice of two daily passenger trains, both westward and eastward.

Between Chicago and St Paul the routes of the *Empire Builder* and the *Western Star* were on the Chicago, Burlington & Quincy lines, and between St Paul and Seattle they were on the Great Northern lines. Between Spokane and Portland, cars from both trains were part of connecting routes of the Spokane, Portland & Seattle Railway.

When the initial transcontinental streamliner fleet took over the *Empire Builder* name in 1947, another famous Great Northern train name was revived. The *Oriental Limited* had first become a Great Northern name in 1905, when the train began operating as a vital link in trade with the Orient in the empire-building era of Jim Hill. New equipment was added in 1924 and in 1931, two years after the first fleet bearing the *Empire Builder* title went into operation. The *Oriental Limited* was 'honorably discharged' as a name train, and remained unused until 1947, when it was reassigned to the six non-streamliner trains, which since 1929 had operated as the first-generation *Empire Builders*. When the fleet of *Empire Builders* that was new in 1947—the second-generation of that train name—was renamed as the *Western Star* in 1951, the latter took over the run and schedule of the *Oriental Limited*, and the *Oriental Limited* name was dropped.

In June 1960, three additional and completely new streamliners, each with five cars and diesel power, all began operating on faster schedules than previously in effect. These new trains were the twin *Internationals*, that made round trips be-

tween Seattle and Vancouver, British Columbia, and the *Red River*, which operated between St Paul and Grand Forks, North Dakota.

The Great Northern, publicizing the fact that its route touched the edge of Montana's Glacier National Park and other similar natural wonders, took most of its car names from the rugged geography of its territory, stressing glaciers, rivers and mountain passes—*Big Horn Pass, Bad Axe River, Blackfoot Glacier, Bois de Sioux River, Chumstick River, Firebrand Pass, Gunsight Pass, Hanging Glacier, Kintla Glacier* and *Lewis and Clark Pass.*

The *Empire Builder* passenger service was abandoned by Burlington Northern after the 1970 merger that brought together the Chicago, Burlington & Quincy with the Great Northern and the Northern Pacific. However, when Amtrak resumed passenger service on American railroad lines in 1971, the name *Empire Builder* was assigned to the Amtrak route that used the same tracks as those of the original Great Northern *Empire Builder.* The Amtrak *Empire Builder* completed the 2217-mile run from Chicago to Seattle in 44 hours.

Also owned by Jim Hill during its formative years, the Northern Pacific Railway paralleled the Great Northern's Chicago to the Pacific route, running several hundred miles south, although both roads served Minneapolis/St Paul and Spokane.

The Northern Pacific Railway's deluxe *North Coast Limited* crossed two-thirds of the width of the continent through the central Northwest in a day and a half. The *North Coast Limited* had something brand-new—a Vista-Dome sleeping car, the first of its kind ever built. It is, in fact and effect, a glorified upstairs sun deck for the occupants of 12 private rooms on the first floor.

Better than almost any other train, this semi-private dome car conveyed the utter luxury of lounging under the glass, in air conditioned sunshine with one's morning coffee and newspaper, listening to soft music and watching the scenery unfold hour after hour—while somebody else did the driving. By early spring 1956, there were four Vista-Domes on

Above: **The early days of a renowned classic: The Union Pacific's *Los Angeles Limited*, circa 1928. It was only one star in the galaxy of 'City' trains operated by the Union Pacific. This is the same train as is seen on page 73.**

each *North Coast Limited*, two of them on sleepers, part of a multimillion-dollar passenger improvement program even then in progress on the Northern Pacific. However, it would never be completed. By 1970, this luxury passenger service was gone and the Northern Pacific name was lost in a merger with the Burlington. The flagship of the Northern Pacific, this streamliner actually operated for part of its route under the motive power of the Chicago, Burlington & Quincy from Chicago to St Paul, while the Northern Pacific hauled the gleaming coaches from St Paul to Seattle. Its sister road, the Spokane, Portland & Seattle, operated a spur line of the *North Coast Limited* between Pasco (near Spokane) and Portland. Introduced by Northern Pacific in the early 1950s, the *Mainstreeter* oper-

ated on the 'Main Street of the Northwest,' a route from Fargo, North Dakota to Seattle. In 1888, the Union Pacific-Central Pacific transcontinental route introduced an all-Pullman vestibuled *Golden Gate Special* to the West Coast, which boasted such luxuries as a library, barbershop and bath.

The first vestibules were narrower than those of today, only slightly wider than the end doors of the cars. Following the lead of naming its first transcontinental through train for its destination, the Union Pacific went on to adopt the practice. Among Union Pacific's portfolio of 'destination' trains were the five famous streamliners the *City of Denver*, the *City of Portland*, the *City of St Louis*, the *City of Los Angeles* and the inimitable *City of San Francisco*, which were operated

Below: Pleasant, but reserved, these well-heeled passengers enjoy a trip aboard a classic Union Pacific 'City' train, circa 1959. The top view shows the Astra Dome observation car, while at the bottom we see the 'attractive and restful' Club Lounge car, which provided current magazines, and 'refreshing beverages at the touch of a button.'

jointly with Chicago & North Western and Southern Pacific.

These were by no means the only classic 'destination' trains on the Union Pacific. Among those serving Portland, Oregon, the *Idahoan* ran all the way from North Platte to Portland, the *Portland Rose* ran from Denver and the *Spokane* ran from that Washington city.

The *National Parks Special* ran from Omaha to Denver and the *Yellowstone Special* transported nature-hungry tourists from Salt Lake City to West Yellowstone, Montana.

The *Butte Special* ran from that city—Montana's copper capital—to Salt Lake City.

The Union Pacific's *City of Denver* offered riders a 'railroad cannonball'—a super-fast train. On the *City of Denver*, passengers rode 560 miles in eight hours, for an average of 70 mph—a good speed even on today's interstate highways.

Scenery flashed past in a blur: The station agent's garden beside the Julesburg Station, where flowers bloomed between rows of corn; seas of ripening wheat; miles of beets and factories converting them into sugar; the Rockies dwindling on the far horizon as the train whipped across the Great Plains, until at last they were only a violet haze lined in gold against the setting sun.

In the mid-1950s, the *City of Denver* had the latest innovation in observation cars—an Astra-Dome diner, the first in America and one of 35 new Astra-Domes then being added to Union Pacific streamliners. Also, the steward could

Below: **The Union Pacific's *City of St Louis,* seen here near Granger, Wyoming, in 1954, featured *two* Astra Dome observation cars.**

UNION PACIFIC RAILROAD

Westbound	EQUIPMENT—Continued	Eastbound

★No. 101—STREAMLINER, CITY OF SAN FRANCISCO.
Extra Fare. Daily. Condensed Table A.

Club Car◆.................Chicago to San Francisco. (Radio.)
Standard Sleeping Cars ....Chicago to San Francisco — Drawing-rooms, Compartments, Double Bedrooms, Roomettes, Sections.
Reclining Seat-Leg Rest Coaches..Chicago to San Francisco (all seats reserved).
Cafe Lounge Car...........Chicago to San Francisco—Moderately priced meals and lounge for coach passengers.
Dining Car.................A la carte and club or table d'hote service.

★No. 103—STREAMLINER, CITY OF LOS ANGELES. Extra Fare. Daily. Condensed Table A.

Club Lounge Car ◆........Chicago to Los Angeles. (Bath, Radio.)
Observation-Lounge◆......Chicago to Los Angeles.
Standard Sleeping Cars....Chicago to Los Angeles — Drawing - rooms, Compartments, Bedrooms, Roomettes, Sections.
Reclining Seat-Leg Rest Coaches..Chicago to Los Angeles (all seats reserved).
Cafe Lounge Car...........Chicago to Los Angeles. (For coach passengers.)
Dining Car ....A la carte and club or table d'hote service.

★No. 105—STREAMLINER, CITY OF PORTLAND. Daily. Condensed Table C.

Club Lounge Car◆........Chicago to Portland. (Bath, Radio.)
Standard Sleeping Cars....Chicago to Portland—2 Drawing-rooms, 4 Compartments, 4 Double Bedrooms
    Chicago to Portland—6-Sections, 6 Roomettes, 4 Double Bedrooms (2 cars).
    Chicago to Seattle—12-Roomettes, 4 Dble. Bedrooms (on 457 to Seattle).
Reclining Seat-Leg Rest Coaches..Chicago to Portland(all seats reserved).
Cafe Lounge Car...........Chicago to Portland. Moderately priced meals; lounge for coach passengers.
Dining Car.................A la carte and club or table d'hote service.

★No. 111—STREAMLINER, CITY OF DENVER. Daily Condensed Table E

Club Lounge Car◆..Chicago to Denver—(Radio.)
Observation Sleeping Car..Chicago to Denver—6 Double Bedrooms.
Standard Sleeping Cars...Chicago to Denver—Drawing-room, Compts., Bedrooms, Roomettes, Sections (4 cars).
Reclining Seat Coaches ....Chicago to Denver — (2 Cars). (All seats reserved.)
Dining Car ....A la carte and club or table d'hote service.

★No. 401—Daily. Condensed Table L.

Standard Sleeping Cars.....Portland to Seattle—10-Sections, Drawing-room, Compartment. (2 Cars.)
    Portland to Seattle—12-Sections, D.R.
    Portland to Tacoma—10-Sec., D.R., Compt.
Sleepers open at Portland 930 p.m; parked at destination until 800 a.m.
Reclining Seat Coaches ....Portland to Seattle.

★No. 407—Daily. Condensed Table L.

Standard Sleeping Car.....San Francisco to Seattle — 22 Roomettes. (Car 122.) (S.P. No. 12 south of Portland.)
    San Francisco to Seattle—6 Dble. Bedrooms, 10 Roomettes. (Cars 123-124.) (S. P. 12 south of Portland.)
    San Francisco to Seattle — 4 Compartments, 4 Double Bedrooms, 2 Drawing-rooms. (Car 125.) (S. P. No 12 south of Portland.)
Parlor Car...............Portland to Seattle. (R. R. owned.)
Reclining Seat Coaches....Portland to Seattle.
Dining Car ....Serving necessary meals en route.

★No. 457—Daily—Streamliner. Table 5.

Astra Dome Obs.-Lounge..Portland to Seattle. (For parlor and sleeping car passengers only.)
Parlor Car................Portland to Seattle. (R.R. owned.)
Astra Dome Room Parlor Car..Portland to Seattle. (R.R. owned)— 8 Duplex Roomette, 3 Compts., 2 D.R.
Standard Sleeping Car.....Chicago to Seattle—12 Roomettes, 4 Double Bedrooms (No. 105 to Portland).
Astra Dome Coach,.......Portland to Seattle (all seats reserved).
Reclining Seat Coaches ...Portland to Seattle (not reserved).
Astra Dome Dining Car....Portland to Seattle.

★No. 459—Daily. Table 5.

Parlor Car (R. R. owned)...Portland to Seattle.
Standard Sleeping Car .....St. Louis to Seattle—6-Sections, 6 Roomettes, 4 Dble. Bedrooms. Nos. 9-11 to Portland.
Reclining Seat Coaches ....Portland to Seattle.
Dining Car.................Serving necessary meals en route.

★No. 102—STREAMLINER, CITY OF SAN FRANCISCO.
Extra Fare. Daily. Condensed Table B.

Club Car◆.................San Francisco to Chicago. (Radio.)
Standard Sleeping Cars ....San Francisco to Chicago — Drawing-rooms, Compartments, Double Bedrooms, Roomettes, Sections.
Reclining Seat-Leg Rest Coaches..San Francisco to Chicago (all seats reserved).
Cafe Lounge Car...........San Francisco to Chicago—Moderately priced meals and lounge for coach passengers.
Dining Car.................A la carte and club or table d'hote service.

★No. 104—STREAMLINER, CITY OF LOS ANGELES. Extra Fare. Daily. Condensed Table B.

Club Lounge Car◆........Los Angeles to Chicago. (Bath, Radio.)
Observation-Lounge◆ .....Los Angeles to Chicago.
Standard Sleeping Cars....Los Angeles to Chicago — Drawing - rooms, Compartments, Bedrooms, Roomettes, Sections.
Reclining Seat-Leg Rest Coaches..Los Angeles to Chicago (all seats reserved).
Cafe Lounge Car...........Los Angeles to Chicago. (For coach passengers.)
Dining Car.................A la carte and club or table d'hote service.

★No. 106—STREAMLINER, CITY OF PORTLAND. Daily. Condensed Table D.

Club Lounge Car◆....Portland to Chicago. (Bath, Radio.)
Standard Sleeping Cars.....Portland to Chicago—2 Drawing-rooms, 4 Compartments, 4 Double Bedrooms.
    Portland to Chicago—6-Sections, 6 Roomettes, 4 Double Bedrooms (2 cars).
    Seattle to Chicago—12-Roomettes, 4 Double Bedrooms (on No. 408 from Seattle).
Reclining Seat-Leg Rest Coaches..Portland to Chicago(all seats reserved).
Cafe Lounge Car...........Portland to Chicago. Moderately priced meals; lounge for coach passengers.
Dining Car................A la carte and club or table d'hote service.

★No 112—STREAMLINER, CITY OF DENVER. Daily. Condensed Table E.

Club Lounge Car◆........Denver to Chicago—(Radio.)
Observation Sleeping Car◆..Denver to Chicago—6 Double Bedrooms.
Standard Sleeping Car......Denver to Chicago—Drawing-room, Compts., Bedrooms, Roomettes, Sections (4 Cars).
Reclining Seat Coaches ....Denver to Chicago — (2 Cars). (All seats reserved.)
Dining Car.................A la carte and club or table d'hote service.

★No. 402—Daily. Condensed Table L.

Standard Sleeping Cars....Seattle to Portland—10 Sections, 1 Drawing-room, 1 Compartment. (2 Cars.)
    Seattle to Portland—12-Sections, D.R.
    Seattle to St. Louis—6-Sections, 6 Roomettes, 4 Double Bedrooms. Nos. 12-10 thru from Portland.
    Tacoma to Portland—10-Sec., D.R., Compt.
Sleepers open at Seattle at 930 p.m.; at Portland until 730 a.m.
Reclining Seat Coaches....Seattle to Portland.

★No. 408—Daily. Condensed Table L.

Standard Sleeping Cars....Seattle to Chicago—12 Roomettes, 4 Double Bedrooms (No. 105 east of Portland).
    Seattle to San Francisco — 22 Roomettes. (Car 112.) (S. P. No. 11 south of Portland.)
    Seattle to San Francisco—6 Dble. Bedrooms, 10 Roomettes. (Cars 113-114.) (S. P. 11 south of Portland.)
    Seattle to San Francisco—4 Compartments, 4 Double Bedrooms, 2 Drawing-rooms. (Car 115.) (S. P. No. 11 south of Portland.)
Parlor Car ....Seattle to Portland. (R. R. owned.)
Reclining Seat Coaches ....Seattle to Portland.
Dining Car............ ....Serving necessary meals en route.

★No. 458—Daily—Streamliner. Condensed Table L.

Astra Dome Obs.-Lounge...Seattle to Portland. (For parlor and sleeping car passengers only.)
Parlor Car ....Seattle to Portland. (R.R. owned.)
Astra Dome Room Parlor Car..Seattle to Portland. (R.R. owned)— 8 Duplex Roomette, 3 Compts., 2 D.R.
Astra Dome Coach.........Seattle to Portland (all seats reserved).
Reclining Seat Coaches.....Seattle to Portland (not reserved).
Astra Dome Dining Car....Seattle to Portland.

★No 460—Daily. Table 5.

Parlor Car................Seattle to Portland. (R.R. owned.)
Reclining Seat Coaches.....Seattle to Portland.
Dining Car.................Serving necessary meals en route.

◆ *Club lounge cars are for the exclusive use of standard sleeping car passengers.*

★ **Regularly Assigned Through Cars Air-Conditioned.**

Facing page: **Compare this 1928 view of a Union Pacific club car on the *Los Angeles Limited* to the Club Lounge car, circa 1959, seen on page 70. This is the same train as seen on page 69.**

telephone the engineer and keep passengers posted on their speed during dinner. With the chicken soup came the first bulletin: 75.8 mph. With the salad, the train rached 77.4 mph, with the grilled mountain trout, 79.2 mph. Finally, with the strawberry shortcake, and for 95 miles thereafter, the *City of Denver*'s speed never dropped below 80 mph.

Among the great 'named routes' few were so powerful, and so pretentious in their wielding of their power, than the *City of San Francisco*, an enormous, gleaming classic that ran between Chicago and its namesake by the Golden Gate. The 39-hour trip was only one

night. The *City of San Francisco* was such a haughty grande dame that she was too massive for one railroad to handle. As noted above, the Southern Pacific, the Union Pacific and the Milwaukee Road all played a role in pulling her for part of her journey.

She was to the rails what the *Titanic* had been to the waves: the largest, most beautiful, fastest, most elegant and modern piece of machinery in a century just into its second generation of idolizing such technology.

She represented not the overstuffed velvet, carved ivory and inlaid wood luxury of the grand Victorian era steam trains, but the flawless fit of form to function, of sleek cocktail gowns in an Art Deco lounge. Fred Astaire could have danced through her tavern car on its semi-circular, chrome-trimmed tables over crescent leather booths—Bauhaus in motion. Her power units, comprising the longest locomotive ever built, consisted of six 900-horsepower, 12-cylinder diesels, the most powerful in the world, capable of hurtling 600 tons of silver voracity at speeds reaching 110 mph. Her trip from Chicago to San Francisco epitomized style.

Her cars bore the names of famed San Francisco locales: *Market Street* and *Portsmouth Square, Seal Rock, Chinatown* and *Twin Peaks*, the *Presidio, Telegraph Hill, Union Square*, and *Mission Dolores*. Passengers could take a drink in the *Nob Hill* amid the soft glow of blonde brass fixtures and put their dry martinis down on circular, mirrored cocktail tables in the *Embarcadero*.

At 9:55 am, the *City of San Francisco* was on her way, crawling past the Chicago stockyards and soon the farmlands, the trees like starving mendicants, the cattle like flies on a card table, through the slowly evaporating Great Plains. On toward the immense sky she glided, and everything else slid behind. The *City of San Francisco* continued to make her transcontinental run—to the San Francisco World's Fair of 1939-1940— and all through the war years. In 1952, she became snowbound on Donner Pass on the California side of the Sierra Nevada, but all remained congenial and there was no loss of life.

Ultimately, however, the grande dame began to grow dowdy, and those who would have once made the trip no other way, now took an airplane. Amtrak's current service on the route is the *California Zephyr*.

THE PACIFIC COAST TRAINS

While there were many classic trains that could take you *to* the Pacific Coast—the *Empire Builder* to Seattle or the *Super Chief* to Los Angeles—the coast itself belonged to the Southern Pacific. Though the Southern Pacific operated its classic *Sunset* across the southern edge of America from Los Angeles to New Orleans, and it helped bring the fabled *City of San Francisco* in from Chicago, Southern Pacific 'owned' the coast with its fleet of *Daylights* and *Starlights*. In 1937, the Southern Pacific introduced the first fabulous *Daylight*, which made the picturesque run down the Pacific coastline from San Francisco to Los Angeles. The

Below: Arguably the most beautiful steam train of her era, Southern Pacific's *Daylight* was the preeminent West Coast train from the 1930s through the 1950s. Actually, she was two trains, with *Coast* and *Shasta* prefixes, and she had sisters known as *Starlights*.

Above: The Southern Pacific's *Coast Daylight*, northbound between Los Angeles and San Francisco, just a little south of San Luis Obispo, circa 1936.

Today, Amtrak operates the same service as the *Coast Starlight* with a run all the way to Seattle. North of Los Angles, the route is by daylight. North of San Francisco, by starlight.

Daylight color scheme of red, orange and black lateral stripes was found on all the train's 12 cars, as well as the sleek, streamlined 4-8-4 oil-burning steam locomotive that invariably headed the *Coast* and *Valley Daylight*s in their heyday. There was also the *Shasta Daylight*, which connected Seattle to San Francisco.

Streaking along one of its several routes, the *Daylight* trains were often compared to 'landlocked comets with long, luminous tails of fire.' The last thing bystanders saw of the train as it flashed by was the signature red neon 'Daylight' logo on the rounded tail of its rearmost car.

Accommodations were of the utmost refinement, from the painted trim of slender leaf-and-stalk borders with tiny quatrefoil motifs, to the soft velour upholstery and the clean, Bauhaus-inspired lines of the cars. In addition to a cabin sleeper car, there was a diner, a lounge/observation car with large windows and rotating, tiltable seats, and section sleeper cars with amazingly luxurious convertible upper and lower berths, shielded for privacy by satiny curtains. There were also day cars with large windows and recliner seats.

The observation/lounge car rode at the end of the train, and featured large windows and a panoramic field of vision out the rounded rear windows at the end of the car. One could take a shower on board if one wanted, and there was every kind of amenity for carrying out leisure activities or company business.

The cars were very Bauhaus, with a touch of Art Deco—the decor was what one would expect in a luxury hotel—and meals could be taken either in the passenger cars or in the diner, which featured shining, white linens and silver tableware buffed to a soft, lustrous tone. This was complete with a full complement of gastronomic delights that were represented in smaller portions on the children's menu. As was the case aboard America's other great streamliners, the *Daylight*'s *chef de train* had a fully equipped kitchen with which to please the passengers' palates.

In the golden age of rail travel, from the late 1930s to the late 1950s, the *Coast Daylight* departed San Francisco at 8:00 am for Los Angeles. From San Francisco, the *Coast Daylight* passed through the sunny, fertile reaches of the Salinas Valley. Then the train went upgrade into the rugged Santa Lucia Mountains, breached the Cuesta Pass, and coming downgrade, rounded a horseshoe curve into San Luis Obispo. From San Luis Obispo to Santa Barbara, the *Coast Daylight* ran along California's magnificent coastline, where the Pacific Ocean sculpts the western edge of the North American continent.

Rugged coastal hills, magnificent rock cliffs, sandy beaches and Southern California flora combined with the awesome grandeur of the Pacific Ocean made this

leg of the *Coast Daylight* route one of the most spectacular in the world.

From Santa Barbara, the train bore inland once more, rising up the western flanks of the Tehachapi Mountains to Santa Susana Pass, and coming down into the San Fernando Valley, pulling into the mecca of movie-making, Los Angeles, that evening.

Over the years, the *Daylight* name was actually applied to a number of Southern Pacific routes offered to the public by the Southern Pacific Railroad. Passengers electing to voyage south from Portland, Oregon on the *Cascade Daylight*—or by connecting service, from Seattle, Washington—could go all the way to Los Angeles, and had a choice of itineraries.

Among those were routes named for their California itinerary. One was an inland route that took its passengers down the San Joaquin Valley, and the other was a coastal route that provided spectacular vistas of the coastal mountains and shoreline. The *Daylight*s that took these routes were known respectively as the *Valley Daylight* and the *Coast Daylight*. Passengers also had a choice of taking the *San Joaquin Daylight* inland through the agriculturally picturesque San Joaquin Valley, or the spectacular *Coast Daylight* from San Francisco to Los Angeles.

In 1949, the Southern Pacific expanded its popular *Daylight* schedules. The *Shasta Daylight* and its predominantly night-running twin, the *Shasta Starlight*,

were introduced on the line from Portland to San Francisco. These trains made the run south in 16.5 hours. In the morning light, the *Shasta Daylight* headed out of Portland, moving out through the Coast Range foothills. The train might be full of businessmen and that unique brand of optimistic young couples—which the advertisers had done everything to persuade of their services—as well as older families out for a lark. Soon the windows of the swivel-seat-equipped observation coaches were full of Pacific Northwest verdure. Hillsides and evergreens, and the occasional glimpse of the meandering Willamette River, formed a pleasant background for one's reflections as the train eased itself into the first leg of its journey.

Just before 9:00 am, the train pulled into Salem, Oregon, the state capital, which like Portland is located on the Willamette River. Small, scenic stops like this helped to add additional variety to the journey to San Francisco. The stops along the line to the California border included Albany, Eugene and Klamath Falls.

The mountainous forest land, the Klamath Lake panorama and Klamath Falls would offer scenes of great natural beauty, as would the awesome spectacle of Mount Shasta rising out of the foothills to the left of the train, dwarfing primordial evergreen forests. Not long afterward, the train headed into Dunsmuir, California, late in the afternoon. The *Day-*

Above: A contemporary view of Amtrak's *Coast Starlight* northbound between Los Angeles and San Francisco, just a little south of San Luis Obispo.

You will note that this train was photographed over half a century later in virtually the same place from virtually the same vantage point as the *Coast Daylight* on the facing page.

light then flew on through the fertile expanses of the Sacramento Valley, running fast and true for the Bay Area and San Francisco. As night began to fall, and the miles ticked by with the steady rhythms of wheels on track, the streamliner would pull into Oakland and passengers would be ferried into San Francisco.

Rail travel in the United States, especially in California, suffered tremendously from competition with automobiles and airplanes in the mid-1950s

through the 1960s, and Southern Pacific was anxious to shed its passenger service. On 1 May 1971, Amtrak assumed control of the Southern Pacific's passenger lines, trimming them severely. The once-proud *Daylight*s and *Starlight*s were consolidated into a single Seattle to Los Angeles service, which took the name *Coast Starlight*.

Today, this train offers both cabin and coach accommodations. Amtrak cabins are of four types—the premier setup being a two-berth unit, convertible for day

use, with its own bathroom and shower. The least luxurious cabin accommodation is a convertible day/night room, with toilet and washroom facilities at the end of the car. Amtrak's *Coast Starlight* also offers a high-level diner, and an observation car with a bar and entertainment such as recorded music and motion pictures. This train runs a daily schedule of 32 hours and 50 minutes from Seattle to Los Angeles, and takes five minutes more to run the return trip. The *Coast Starlight* is not, however, the only service still offered by Amtrak in the Golden State. The classic *San Diegan* service still runs from Santa Barbara to San Diego via Union Station in Los Angeles. The *San Joaquin* also still runs from Oakland to Bakersfield via Merced and Fresno, while the *Capitol* runs between San Jose and Sacramento over the route made famous by Southern Pacific's *Senator* and all the great transcontinental trains from the very first run in May 1869 up through, and including, today's *California Zephyr*.

Below: **Number 4449, the last of the classic Lima-built *Daylight* steam trains, still operates on the West Coast, but not in scheduled service, and no longer by Southern Pacific.**

INDEX